FROM
SCRIPT TO PRINT

From
SCRIPT TO PRINT

An Introduction to
Medieval Vernacular Literature

H. J. CHAYTOR, Litt.D.
*Late Master of St. Catharine's College,
Cambridge*

SIDGWICK & JACKSON
LONDON

First published 1945 by W. Heffer & Sons Ltd, Cambridge, England

This edition published 1966

© *W. Heffer & Sons, Ltd*

Rursus, vim et virtutem et consequentias rerum inventarum notare juvat; quae non in aliis manifestius occurrunt, quam in illis tribus quae antiquis incognitae, et quarum primordia, licet recentia, obscura et ingloria sunt: Artis nimirum Imprimendi, Pulveris Tormentarii, et Acus Nauticae. Haec enim tria rerum faciem et statum in orbe terrarum mutaverunt.

Bacon, *Nov. Org.* Lib. 1, 129.

*Printed in Great Britain by
Fletcher & Son Ltd, Norwich for
Sidgwick and Jackson Ltd
1 Tavistock Chambers, Bloomsbury Way
London, W.C.1*

To

MY WIFE

CONTENTS

CONTENTS

PREFACE

Some fragments of this book have already appeared in the *Modern Language Review*, *Modern Languages*, and the *Bulletin of the John Rylands Library*. The only abbreviations used in the foot-notes are A.T.F. (Anciens Textes français), *M.L.R.* (*Modern Language Review*) and P.M.L.A. (Publications of the Modern Language Society of America). I have to thank Professors R. A. Williams, E. Vinaver, J. Dechamps, Mr H. S. Bennett and Dr L. C. Harmer, who have read the manuscript, for much valuable criticism and advice. But they are in no degree responsible for the opinions which I have attempted to expound.

H. J. CHAYTOR

CHAPTER I

INTRODUCTION

No one is likely to contest the statement that the invention of printing and the development of that art mark a turning-point in the history of civilisation. Not so readily appreciated is the fact that association with printed matter has changed our views of literary art and style, has introduced ideas concerning originality and literary property of which the age of manuscript knew little or nothing, and has modified the psychological processes by which we use words for the communication of thought. The breadth of the gulf which separates the age of manuscript from the age of print is not always, nor fully, realised by those who begin to read and criticise medieval literature. When we take up a printed edition of a medieval text, provided with an introduction, a critical apparatus of variant readings, notes and glossary, we bring unconsciously to its perusal those prejudices and prepossessions which years of association with printed matter have made habitual. We are liable to forget that we are dealing with the literature of an age when orthographical standards varied and grammatical accuracy was not highly esteemed, when language was fluid and was not necessarily regarded as a mark of nationality, when style meant the observance of fixed and complicated rules of rhetoric. To copy and circulate another man's book might be regarded as a meritorious action in the age of manuscript; in the age of print, such action results in law suits and damages. Writers who wish to derive profit by amusing a public now write for the most part in prose; until the middle of the thirteenth century, only verse could obtain a hearing. Hence, if a fair judgment is to be passed upon literary works belonging to the centuries before printing was invented, some effort must be made to realise the extent of the prejudices under which we have grown up, and to resist the involuntary demand that medieval literature must conform to our standards of taste or be regarded as of interest purely antiquarian. In the words of Renan, 'l'essence de la critique est de savoir comprendre des états très différents de celui où nous vivons'.

This book is an attempt to show the importance of the difference between the literary and critical methods of the early middle ages and those of modern times. Any such attempt must necessarily make French literature the point of departure. By the close of the tenth century France had assimilated the Germanic or foreign elements in her population to her own Gallo-Roman culture, and had begun to develop literatures and styles of art which left their mark upon the greater part of Western Europe. This influence was steadily exerted during the next three centuries; feudal nobles began to take an interest in art and literature, when their attention was not occupied by internecine quarrels; town and city life increased in wealth and independence; the influence of the Church and especially of the universities extended far and wide. Students from all parts of Europe came in particular to Paris, attracted by such teachers as Abelard, Albertus Magnus and Thomas Aquinas; Reims, Orléans, Toulouse, Montpellier and many other university towns were constantly visited by foreigners. England and Germany sent many who became well-known names; Adalbert, archbishop of Mayence, Konrad von Wittelsbach of the same town, Otto von Freising, Stephen Langton, Walter Map, Matthew Paris, John of Salisbury, a list that might be vastly extended. Scandinavian students came from Iceland, Denmark and Sweden; at Paris they were included with Hungarians and Slavs in the *provincia non anglicana* of the English 'nation'. Such foreigners helped to spread French culture far and wide; if they came in the first instance to study theology and canon law, it is not to be supposed that music and poetry escaped their notice or that they remained ignorant of the language of the country. French teachers, craftsmen and architects found work abroad; the crusades and the practice of pilgrimage produced exchanges of interests and ideals with the result that the stamp of French culture became everywhere apparent in vernacular literatures. Of England there is no need to speak; French influence had entered this country before 1066. The German Minnesänger learned and borrowed much from the troubadours, and translated or imitated the *chansons de geste et d'aventure* of Northern France. Italian literature owed much to both Northern and Southern France. In France, Spain and Portugal found models both for lyric and epic poetry; the *Poema del Cid* is rich in French turns of thought and expression. Haakon IV of Norway (1217–1263) used French *chansons de geste* to serve as a means of Christian propaganda.

All this imaginative literature, *chansons de geste, chansons courtoises,* verse and prose romances, which was read or heard from one end of Europe to the other, is marked by two essential characteristics; it is based upon religious sentiment and belief, and the ideal upheld is that of the knightly virtues. The knight is the vassal of God, as of his earthly overlord, and earthly love, in its highest manifestation, is a reflection of love divine. Medieval French literature is the expression of a feudal and Christian society, and as European society in the twelfth and thirteenth centuries was based upon the same principles, nations were prepared to welcome French literature as expressing their own social feelings and aspirations. Hence any generalisations that may be based upon French literary methods and productions will probably be found true in some respects of other European nationalities, until the middle of the thirteenth century, when the confusion of the Hundred Years' War brought about a change of conditions and a diminution of French influence. But France was first in the field of literature, and all European literatures in greater or less degree are indebted to France for inspiration and stimulus.

Medieval literature produced little formal criticism in our sense of the term. If an author wished to know whether his work was good or bad, he tried it on an audience; if it was approved, he was soon followed by imitators. But authors were not constrained by models or systems, and independence or originality could enlarge and decorate any ground-plan that had found general acceptance. Development proceeded by trial and error, the audience being the means of experiment. The audience wanted a story with plenty of action and movement; the story, as a rule, showed no great command of character drawing; this was left to the reciter for portrayal by change of voice and gesture. The story might contain or depend upon the most improbable coincidences or the wildest historical anachronisms; the audience would swallow them without demur. Unity of action could be provided by the use of allegory, a method borrowed from the schools of biblical inter-pretation, or by emphasis upon the love-motive, to which vast im-portance was attached. So, to appreciate the medieval narrative poem, we have to bear in mind that the women are peerless beauties, and the men are heroes dauntless amid perils arising from foes often more than human, and that the story will be a failure, unless these are provided in adequate quantity and energetic intensity.

Little attention was paid to vernacular literature by the humanists such as John of Salisbury, John of Garland and others of their kind. Their criticism was chiefly directed to stimulating the love of sound classical literature and to improving the quality of contemporary Latin prose. The precepts and the recipes of the medieval rhetoricians who wrote in Latin were familiar to many writers of vernacular tongues who had probably studied rhetoric in their early years; but they naturally modified what principles they had learnt, in order to suit the taste of the audiences to whom they appealed. The elaborate rules, for instance, concerning the arrangement of matter and the art of narrative were constantly disregarded by writers of imaginative literature, and their works in consequence seem to us to lack a sense of proportion and perspective; but they wrote for recitation, and for recitation at intervals of time; it was thus possible and even necessary to satisfy popular taste by the introduction of episodes and descriptions which contribute but little to the action of the plot or to the characterisation of the actors. It was not possible for a twelfth-century audience to view a *roman d'aventure* as a whole, unless they were possessed of extraordinary patience and unless the reciter or reader were of extraordinary stamina; they received the story in instalments; we can sit and read it at our leisure and turn back to previous pages at our will. In short, the history of the progress from script to print is a history of the gradual substitution of visual for auditory methods of communicating and receiving ideas. It is not a history that can ever be written in full; we are largely dependent upon hints and indications, between which the gaps may be considerable, while the difference between the faculties of individuals makes generalisation hazardous. But to disregard the matter and to criticise medieval literature as though it had just been issued by the nearest circulating library is a sure and certain road to a misconception of the medieval spirit.

CHAPTER II

READING & WRITING

I N the medieval world, those who could read or write were the few, and it is likely that most of them did not read or write with our methods or with our facility. In order to gain some idea of the difficulties under which they laboured, it is necessary to consider what mental processes are involved in the understanding of spoken or written speech. Psychologists are by no means agreed upon this subject, but most of them would probably accept the following account of its implications.

When we hear the phrase, 'give me that book', the word 'book' is recognised as a familiar collocation of sounds; in psychological language, we gain an 'acoustic image' which experience enables us to identify. This experience includes not only the recognition of particular sounds, but also takes into account pitch, emphasis and intonation; the individual word 'book', spoken in isolation, would evoke an image, but would convey no information stimulating to action, unless such information were provided by gesture or emphasis or intonation. In some languages the isolated word has different meanings, according to the 'tone' used by the speaker. All languages are, to some extent, 'tone' languages; the simple phrase, 'Good morning', may mean, according to the manner of its utterance, 'I'm delighted to see you', or, 'Here's that infernal bore again'; it may mean, 'Thank goodness, he's going', or 'Come again when you can'.

Experience, therefore, takes into account other matters than the sounds which compose an individual word; but for the purpose of this analysis, we confine our attention to the word as such. The acoustic image may be translated into the visual image of a book, and if the hearer is illiterate, this is probably the end of the process. If the hearer can read, he will substitute for the visual image of a book the printed word 'book', and in either case there may be a half-felt tendency to articulate the word, a feeling known to psychology as a 'kinesthetic' or 'speech-motor' image.

When, therefore, a child is learning to read, his task is to construct from printed symbols an acoustic image which he can recognise. When recognition has been achieved, he pronounces the word, not only for the satisfaction of his teacher, but also because he cannot himself understand the printed symbols without transforming them into sounds; he can read only aloud. When he can read faster than he can speak, pronunciation becomes a rapid muttering, and eventually ceases entirely. When this stage has been reached, the child has substituted a visual for an acoustic image, and so long as he continues to be dependent upon printed matter, as most of us are, this condition is never likely to change. When we read, the visual image of the printed word-form instantaneously becomes an acoustic image; kinesthetic images accompany it, and if we are not reading aloud, the combination of the two produces 'inner speech', which, in the case of most people, includes both inner speaking and inner hearing. It may be that inner pronunciation falls below the threshold of consciousness in the case of those greatly occupied with printed matter; but it will rise to the surface, if the individual begins to read a foreign language in a script with which he is not entirely familiar, or to learn by heart a difficult passage which must be orally reproduced verbatim. It is said that some doctors forbid patients with severe throat affections to read, because silent reading provokes motions of the vocal organs, though the reader may not be conscious of them. So also when we speak or write, ideas evoke acoustic combined with kinesthetic images, which are at once transformed into visual word images. The speaker or writer can now hardly conceive of language, except in printed or written form; the reflex actions by which the process of reading or writing is performed have become so 'instinctive' and are performed with such facile rapidity, that the change from the auditory to the visual is concealed from the reader or writer, and makes analysis of it a matter of great difficulty. It may be that acoustic and kinesthetic images are inseparable, and that 'image' as such is an abstraction made for purposes of analysis, but which is non-existent considered in itself and as pure. But whatever account the individual may render of his own mental processes, and most of us are far from competent in this respect, the fact remains that his idea of language is irrevocably modified by his experience of printed matter.

The result is that we cannot think of language without reference to its written or printed form, and many prefer the printed to the written word, because print is clearer to them; it relieves a strain upon the memory and gives time for deliberate consideration.[1] The hearer to whom a letter has been read will ask to see the script, in order to make sure that he has missed no point; he will take notes of a lecture, lest he should forget matters of interest; no policeman is complete without a pencil to lick and a notebook wherein to scrawl. Visualisation can even be an aid to memory; most of us have a clear image, even in advanced age, of certain pages in our first Latin grammar or our first repetition book, and educational writers have begun to realise that the 'lay-out' of the page is almost as important to the learner as the matter which it contains. It is by visual practice that we master the vagaries of English orthography, and so-called bad spellers are often those who are misled by inability to exclude auditory reminiscences; they may be seen, when in doubt, to write down a word on scribbling paper, 'to see how it looks', to recover, that is, a visual memory which has become blurred. Hearing and sight, once disconnected, have become inseparable; when we hear a speaker, the effect of his words is transmitted from the auditory to the visualising capacity, and we see, or can see, the words 'in our mind's eye', whether we wish to take notes or not. And when we read to ourselves, the visual impression is accompanied by an auditory perception; we hear, or can hear, the sentences that we read, and when we compose, we write to the dictation of an inner voice.

'Sound and sight, speech and print, eye and ear have nothing in common. The human brain has done nothing that compares in complexity with this fusion of ideas involved in linking up the two forms of language. But the result of the fusion is that once it is achieved in our early years, we are for ever after unable to think clearly, independently and surely about any one aspect of the matter. We cannot think of sounds without thinking of letters; we believe letters have sounds. We think that the printed page is a picture of what we say, and that the mysterious thing called "spelling" is sacred.... The invention of

1 'Wenn ich einem Deutschen einen Zeitungsartikel oder sonst etwas vorlesen will, dann nimmt er mir das Blatt aus der Hand und sagt: "Gib; ich will's selber lesen." Nur was er schwarz auf weiss gesehen hat, versteht er richtig. Aufs Gehör allein mag er sich nicht verlassen, die Augen müssen mitwirken. Dem Franzosen genügt das Gehör. Um etwas Neues zu erfahren, zieht er das Hören dem Lesen sogar bei weitem vor.' (Paul Distelbarth, *Lebendiges Frankreich*, 1936.)

printing broadcast the printed language and gave to print a degree of authority that it has never lost.'[1]

Children can learn languages more easily than adults, because they can concentrate wholly upon audition and are not hampered by habits of visualisation; just for that reason, they forget almost as rapidly as they learn, unless they are in continual contact with the language concerned. For the adult to return to the infantile stage of simple auditory perception is a task of extraordinary difficulty for those who are obliged to face it, as, for instance, the missionary who proposes to reduce an unwritten language to writing. He must first learn it as a spoken tongue until he is so fully master of it as to be able to decompose the words he has heard into their component sounds and find a symbol to represent each sound, in fact, to form an alphabet. But in this task, he will be continually hampered by the fact that he has been accustomed to regard language as visualised in the garb of a written orthography.

But when the ordinary well-educated man is learning a new language and hears an unfamiliar word, supposing him to have reached the stage of ability to separate the words of a new language, his instinctive inquiry is, how is it spelt? what does it look like in writing? from what is it derived or with what known words is it cognate? Given this help, he can associate the new acquisition with his previous experience and has a chance of making a permanent addition to his vocabulary. But if he has to depend upon audition alone, he will certainly forget the new word, unless circumstances oblige him to make use of it forthwith and frequently. Such is the consequence of association with print; in printer's ink auditory memory has been drowned and visual memory has been encouraged and strengthened.

Thought, in the full sense of the term, is hardly possible without words. When ideas rise above the threshold of consciousness, they are formulated by the mind in words; accustomed as we are to impart and receive information by means of language, we inevitably follow the same method when we are occupied by mental consideration; we discuss a matter with ourselves as we might discuss it with an interlocutor, and such discussion cannot be conducted without the use of words. Hence, until ideas can be formulated in words, they can hardly be regarded as fully conceived. Here, an objection is raised: unless the

[1] A. Lloyd James, *Our Spoken Language*, London, 1938, p. 29.

thinker possesses words, he cannot think; but, unless he has thought, he cannot possess words; how then was the process begun? Did ideas precede language, or is capacity for speech innate and awaiting only the stimulus of ideas provoked by external accident, in order to break into action? In other words, did the hen or the egg come first? This question has interested those concerned with the origins of language, but it does not affect the reality of inner speech as the method of inner thought. This reality has been admitted from the days of Homer to our own time. Odysseus, alone upon his raft and confronted by the rising storm, 'in trouble spake to his own great soul' for some twenty hexameter lines; and a public-house orator, describing his domestic troubles, will say: 'then I sez to meself, this 'ere 'as got ter stop', and will conclude his catastrophic narrative, 'so I sez to meself, I must 'ave a pint and I comes rahnd 'ere'. If the thinker is illiterate, the images that arise in his mind will be auditory; if he is literate, they will be visual; in either case, immediate vocal expression can be given to them, if necessary.

As has been said, this vocal expression is necessary to children who are learning to read or to inexperienced adults; they cannot understand the written or printed symbols without transforming them into audible sounds. Silent reading comes with practice, and when practice has made perfect, we do not realise the extent to which the human eye has adapted itself to meet our requirements. If we take a line of printed matter, cut it lengthways in half, so that the upper half of the lettering is exactly divided from the lower half, and then hand the slips to two friends, we shall probably find that the man with the upper half will read the line more easily than the man with the lower half. The eye of the practised reader does not take in the whole of the lettering, but merely so much as will suggest the remainder to his experienced intelligence. Similarly, if we listen to a speaker with a difficult delivery, we instinctively supply syllables and even words which we have failed to hear. Nor does the eye halt at each separate word. When we read our own language, we halt at a point in the line, notice a few letters on either side of it, and proceed to another halting point; the eye has not seen the whole formation of every word, but has seen enough to infer the meaning of the passage. Hence the difficulty of proof-reading; our usual method of reading allows us to pass over misprints, because we see enough of any one word to take its correctness for granted. The number of these halting-places will vary with the nature of the matter to be read; in a foreign language they will be more numerous than when we are concerned with our own familiar tongue, and if we are reading a manuscript in a crabbed hand with many contractions, we shall be forced to proceed almost letter by letter.

Very different was the case of the medieval reader. Of the few who could read, few were habitual readers; in any case, the ordinary man of our own times probably sees more printed and written matter in a week than the medieval scholar saw in a year. Nothing is more alien to medievalism than the modern reader, skimming the headlines of a newspaper and glancing down its columns to glean any point of interest, racing through the pages of some dissertation to discover whether it is worth his more careful consideration, and pausing to gather the argument of a page in a few swift glances. Nor is anything more alien to modernity than the capacious medieval memory which, untrammelled by the associations of print, could learn a strange language with ease and by the methods of a child, and could retain in memory and reproduce lengthy epic and elaborate lyric poems. Two points, therefore, must be emphasised at the outset. The medieval reader, with few exceptions, did not read as we do; he was in the stage of our muttering childhood learner; each word was for him a separate entity and at times a problem, which he whispered to himself when he had found the solution; this fact is a matter of interest to those who edit the writings which he produced.[1] Further, as readers were few and hearers numerous, literature in its early days was produced very largely for public recitation; hence, it was rhetorical rather than literary in character, and rules of rhetoric governed its composition.

Even a superficial acquaintance with medieval literature will show that its exponents continued the custom of public recitation common in classical times.[2] The complaint of Juvenal's opening satire may well have been repeated in medieval times. Authors read their works in

---

1 Under the Rule of St Benedict, each monk was to receive a book from the library: 'accipiant omnes singulos codices de bibliotheca, quos per ordinem ex integra legant; qui codices in caput Quadragesimae dandi sunt' (*Regula*, cap. XLVIII). No limit of time was set and the books appear to have been returned at the beginning of the succeeding Lent. A year for one book seems a generous allowance; but the slowness of the medieval reader is obvious from this instance.

2 An article entitled *Oral Delivery in the Middle Ages*, by Ruth Crosby (*Speculum*, XI (1936), pp. 88 ff.), discusses this subject with a large number of references, chiefly to Old French and Middle English literature.

public, as this was the only way in which they could publish them; Giraldus Cambrensis read his *Topographia Hiberniae* before a public meeting at Oxford for three days in succession to different audiences. Private readings to a circle of friends were more common than these set performances, and naturally increased as manuscripts were multiplied and education spread. It was a public perhaps more eager to hear stories than to gather information that supported the numerous professional story-tellers, the minstrels and jongleurs who went about the countries and were as necessary to medieval society as was their counterpart in Arab civilisation. They performed the business of providing amusement which has been taken over by the radio and the cinema at the present time. Authors expressly state that their work is intended to be recited; a glance at such a work as *Les Incipit des Poèmes français antérieurs au XVIe Siècle* (A. Långfors, Paris, 1917) will provide numerous statements and exhortations of this kind. 'Or oez tuit coumunement', 'Or oiez un flabel courtois', 'Or escoutez, grans et menour', 'Or entendez tuit par amor', are almost conventional exordia. So in Spanish:[1]

> Amigos e vassalos de Dios omnipotent,
> Si vos me escuchades por vuestro consiment,
> Querriavos contar un buen aveniment.
>
> (*Milagros de Nuestra Sennora*, vv. 1–3.)

El Libro de Alexandre begins:

> Sennores, se quisierdes mio servicio prender,
> Querriavos de grado servir de mio menester.

La Vida de Santa Maria Egipçiaca:

> Oyt varones, huna razon
> En que non ha ssi verdat non;
> Escuchat de coraçon,
> Si ayades de Dios perdon.

Instruction and amusement may be promised in combination; thus the opening lines of Wace's *Roman de Rou*:

> Pur remembrer des ancesurs
> Les feiz e les diz e les murs,

. . . .

1 For similar cases in the *Poema del Cid*, due to French influence, see Menéndez Pidal, *Poesía Juglaresca*, pp. 330 f. Thus the early Victorian novelist used to apostrophise the 'gentle reader'.

> Deit l'um les livres e les gestes
> E les estoires lire[1] as festes.
> Si escripture ne fust feite
> E puis par clers litte e retraite,
> Mult fussent choses ubliees,
> Ki de viez tens sunt trespassees.

Wace began his *Roman de Brut* with a similar appeal to an audience. The narrative poet is careful to warn his hearers of any transition of the subject-matter, by a summary of what had been said and an announcement of what they were to hear. Thus Chrétien de Troyes (*Cligés*, l. 570):

> Del roi Artu parler ne quier
> A ceste foiz plus longuemant:
> Einçois m'orroiz dire, comant
> Amors les deus amanz travaille.

After relating the birth of Cligés (l. 2382), he proceeds to explain that the child is to be the subject of the poem:

> Nez est Cligés, an cui memoire
> Fu mise an romanz ceste estoire.
> De lui et de son vasselage
> Quant il iert venuz an aage,
>
> .   .   .   .
>
> M'orroiz assez dire et conter.

The jongleur often refers to hearers in the concluding lines of a recitation, as in the *Roman de Horn*, which suggest that he had been reading from a manuscript:

> Seignurs, oi avez le vers del parchemin
> Cum li bers Aaluf est venuz a sa fin.

The *Roman de Fréjus*:

> Ichi est la fin du romanch,
> Pais et salus as escoutans.

Fierabras:

> Bon es d'aquest romans la fi e l'encontrada
> E.l mieg loc e pertot, qui be l'a escoutada.

The introduction of conversations provided opportunities for personification and dramatic delivery; asseverations of the truth of the tale,

1 *lire*=read aloud, as did the Latin *legere*: see p. 15.

reinforced by appeals to heaven, were intended to enlist the interest of the audience, which is encouraged to visualise exciting scenes by the use of 'epideictic' expressions:[1] 'Es vos un angle qui descent de la nue'; 'La veissies un estor esbaudir'. These points alone clearly show that such compositions were not written to be read à la Macaulay, 'with your feet upon the fender'. The whole technique of *chanson de geste, roman d'aventure*, and lyric poem presupposed, as will be seen, a hearing, not a reading public.[2] When culture had reached that stage at which the individual read to himself for his own enjoyment, a different kind of literature was in demand.

The habits of the medieval reader or scribe are well illustrated by a passage in Grimmelshausen's *Simplicissimus* (Book 1, chap. 10); the hero informs us: 'als ich das erstemal den Einsiedel in der Bibel lesen sahe, konnte ich mir nicht einbilden, mit wem er doch ein solch heimlich und meinem Bedünken nach sehr ernstlich Gespräch haben müsste. Ich sahe wohl die Bewegung seiner Lippen, hörte auch das Gebrummel, hingegen aber sahe und hörte ich niemand, der mit ihm redete.' The passage recalls the situation in Acts viii. 30, where Philip hears the eunuch of Candace reading Isaiah with no visible audience. When we encounter anyone poring over a newspaper, and whispering the words to himself as he laboriously spells his way through the sheet, we set him down as uneducated. It is not commonly realised that this was the manner of reading generally practised in the ancient world and during the early days of Christianity. For these periods the case has been fairly well proved by Josef Balogh,[3] who develops the statements made by Eduard Norden (*Die antike Kunstprosa*, Leipzig, 1898); but Balogh provides very little evidence for the medieval period, and draws most of his evidence from patristic literature. This ancient practice was continued in medieval times, until it was killed by the dissemination of printed matter, and the habit of mind which it implies deserves the notice of those who take in hand the editing of medieval texts.

Professor Vinaver (p. 129 n.) contributed to the *Studies presented to*

1 See E. Lommatzsch, *Deiktische Elemente im Altfranzösischen*, in *Hauptfragen der Romanistik*, Festschrift für P. A. Becker, Heidelberg, 1922, pp. 101 ff.

2 See Appendix A.

3 *Voces Paginarum*, Leipzig, Dieterich, 1927, a reprint of two articles in *Philologus*, Band 82, 1926–27, p. 84. Some of the medieval passages here quoted are due to Dr Coulton, who has drawn attention to this subject in his *Five Centuries of Religion* and other works.

M. K. Pope an article upon textual emendation in which he analysed the mental processes incident to the copying of a manuscript, and showed with much penetration how such mistakes as those classified under the names 'homoioteleuton', 'dittography' and similar aberrations can occur. But this ingenious analysis and the diagrams which illustrate it seem to labour under one defect; they assume that the mèdieval scribe adopted exactly the mental attitude that one of ourselves would assume if he were occupied in copying a manuscript for his own purposes. This was certainly not the case, for the reason that we gain the majority of our information and ideas from printed matter, whereas the medieval obtained them orally. He was confronted not by the beautiful productions of a university press, but by a manuscript often crabbed in script and full of contractions, and his instinctive question, when deciphering a text, was not whether he had seen, but whether he had heard this or that word before; he brought not a visual but an auditory memory to his task. Such was the result of his up-bringing; he had learnt to rely on the memory of spoken sounds, not upon the interpretation of written signs. And when he had deciphered a word, he pronounced it audibly.[1]

If the evidence for this habit of mind and action seems scanty, it must be remembered that early testimony is constantly silent upon subjects concerning which we should like to have information, simply because these matters were so universally common as to pass without comment. As evidence falling within medieval times may be quoted the *Rule of St Benedict*, chap. xlviii, which ordered that monks 'post sextam (horam) surgentes a mensa, pausent in lecta sua cum omni silentio; aut forte qui voluerit legere, sibi sic legat ut alium non inquietet', which suggests that the common manner of reading to oneself meant whispering or muttering. Bernard Pez[2] relates of Richalm of Schönthal: 'oftentimes,

1 The process is thus described by a copyist of the eighth century on concluding his work: 'qui scribere nescit nullum putat esse laborem. Tres digiti scribunt, duo oculi vident. Una lingua loquitur, totum corpus laborat, et omnis labor finem habet, et praemium ejus non habet finem' (Wattenbach, *Schriftwesen im Mittelalter*, Leipzig, 1896, p. 495). Three fingers hold the pen, the eyes see the words, the tongue pronounces them as they are written and the body is cramped with leaning over the desk. The scribe is obviously unable to avoid the necessity of pronouncing each word as he deciphers it.

2 G. G. Coulton, *Five Centuries of Religion*, I, p. 38, from Bernard Pez, *Thesaurus anecdotorum novissimus*, 1721, I, part ii, pp. 376 ff.

when I am reading straight from the book and in thought only, as I am wont, they (devils) make me read aloud word by word, that they may deprive me so much the more of the inward understanding thereof, and that I may the less penetrate into the interior force of the reading, the more I pour myself out in exterior speech'. This is the case of a man who is trying to accustom himself to silent reading and has not yet formed the habit. Johannes Busch, a great monastic reformer (1450), received a reply to a letter: 'Predilecte pater Johannes in Windesem! Litera vestra dulciter sonuit in auribus meis.'[1] So Erasmus wrote to the Hungarian Bishop Nicolaus Oláh in 1533: 'Oro ut hanc epistolam legas solus nec huic tabellioni quicquam arcani committas';[2] the reading of a private letter by the recipient might be overheard. *Legere*, *lire*, and *read* might mean to read or to read aloud;[3] the following passage from Johannes Busch shows *legere* as equivalent to *dicere*; the reformer was on a visit of inspection and was catechising certain members of a congregation: 'Tunc dixi, "estis vos bonus christianus, tunc dicatis Pater Noster in teutonico". Qui statim cunctis audientibus legit coram nobis Pater Noster et Ave Maria in bono teutonico. Et dixi, "legatis etiam Credo in Deum". Et legit Credo per totum in bono teutonico satis expresse....Interrogavi in prandio, "quomodo rusticus ille tam formaliter scivit respondere?" Qui dixerunt, quod plebanus eorum ipsis iniunxit, ut nullum secum in tabernis prandere seu convivari permitterent, nisi prius Pater Noster, Ave Maria et Credo in Deum diceret. Et tunc inter se de illis mutuo conferebant et ita ea perfecte dicere et intellegere didicerunt.'[4]

So in *L'Hystore Job*[5] (vv. 1644–1647):

> Quant tu le prophete liras
> tu li orras huquier, au lire,
> le terre trois fies et dire:
> 'Je voel que mes parolles oies.'

1 Johannes Busch, *Chronicon Windeshemense*, von Karl Grube, Halle, 1886, p. 43. But contrast Petrarch, *Epistolae Seniles*, v: 'videntem omnia Deum testor, decies vel eo amplius retentavi ita scriptum mittere, ut, etsi stilus neque aures neque animum, litera saltem oculos oblectaret' (date, 1365).

2 Balogh, p. 239.

3 So also *lesen* in Middle High German can mean *vorlesen* or *vortragen*; e.g. *Meier Helmbrecht*, by Wernher der Gartenaere, l. 74,

> Ez ist wär daz ich iu lise.

4 Busch, p. 442.   5 Ed. R. C. Bates, Yale University Press, 1937.

'When you read the prophet (Jeremiah xxii. 29), you will hear him, as you read, admonish the earth three times and say, etc.' The editor notes 'Lire ici veut dire, sans doute, lecture à haute voix; autrement l'auteur n'aurait pas employé le verbe *ouïr*'. The statement is made to one person and *lire* is used in the same sense as that given by Johannes Busch to *legere*.[1] Bernard of Morlaix or Morval appears to make little difference between *dicere* and *scribere* in the preface to his great poem *De Contemptu Mundi*: 'cum in meditatione mea non paucos dies et noctes exardesceret ignis zeli, tandem accinxi me, et locutus sum in lingua mea quod animo conceptum diu celaveram apud me. Quippe ego sepe ab sponso audieram, sed non exaudieram:—Sonet vox tua in auribus meis...dixi, Domine ut cor meum cogitet ut stilus scribat ut os annuntiet laudem tuam infunde et corde et stilo et ori meo gratiam tuam. Et dixit mihi Dominus: Aperi os tuum et ego adinplebo illud. Aperui igitur os meum, quod implevit Dominus spiritu sapientiae et intellectus, ut per illam vera, per istum perspicuum dicerem.' The following[2] is an obvious case of one who reads aloud to himself:

> And ek in other wise also
> Ful ofte time it falleth so,
> Min Ere with a good pitaunce
> Is fedd of redinge of romaunce
> Of Ydoine and of Amadas,
> That whilom weren in mi cas,
> And eke of othere mony a score,
> That loveden longe er I was bore,
> For whan I of here loves rede,
> Min Ere with the tale I fede.

There were undoubtedly cases of silent reading; the well-known instance of Ambrosius described by St Augustine (*Confessions*, Book VI, chap. 3) is perhaps repeated in Chaucer (*The Hous of Fame*, II, 148):

> Thou goost hoom to thy hous anoon,
> And, also domb as any stoon,
> Thou sittest at another boke,
> Til fully daswed is thy loke.

1 So *leer* is used in Old Spanish: see examples in R. Menéndez Pidal, *Cantar de Mío Cid*, Madrid, 1908, I, p. 10.

2 Gower, *Confessio Amantis*, VI, 875. Quoted by Ruth Crosby, *Oral Delivery in the Middle Ages*, in *Speculum*, XI, part i (January 1936), pp. 88–110. For further instances, see Appendix B.

Thomas Hoccleve, who spent most of his life as a writer in the Privy Seal Office, defended his occupation against those who thought writing an easy occupation as compared with manual labour, in his translation of the *De Regimine Principum*, which he made in 1411–12 (see E.E.T.S. Extra Series, LXI, 1892):

> A writer mot thre thynges to hym knytte,
> And in those may be no disseverance;
> Mynde, ee and hand, non may fro othir flitte,
> But in them mot be joint contynuance.
> The mynd, al hoole withouten variance,
> On the ee and hand awayte mot alway,
> And thei two eek on hym; it is no nay.
>
> Whoso schal wryte, may nat holde a tale
> With hym and hym, ne synge this ne that;
> But alle his wittes grete and smale
> Ther must appere, and halden them therat,
> And syn he speke may, ne synge nat,
> But bothe two he needes moot forbere:
> His labour to hym is the alengere.

Hoccleve, as a professional writer, had probably learnt the habit of silent reading. The hired *scriptor* or scrivener began to supplement or to replace the monastic scribe at an early date; St Albans made regulations for the employment of such professionals before the middle of the thirteenth century; in the late fourteenth century the York scriveners formed a guild of their own. In university towns the scrivener could make a steady income; those who were under university control were occupied with books on law, theology or medicine, and authors of *belles-lettres* had to content themselves with scriveners not thus occupied, who were less reliable than the more professional class.[1]

But such practised readers were regarded as exceptional. Further evidence may be seen in the strict rule of silence in the medieval scriptorium. Alcuin wished to protect the copyists of religious texts in the scriptorium at Tours from any distraction of the kind:

> Hic sedeant sacrae scribentes famina legis,
> Nec non sanctorum dicta sacrata patrum;
> His interserere caveant sua frivola verbis,
> Frivola ne propter erret et ipsa manus.

1 See Wattenbach, pp. 395 ff.

Correctosque sibi quaerant studiose libellos,
Tramite quo recto penna volantis eat.
Per cola distinguant proprios et commata sensus,
Et punctos ponant ordine quosque suo,
Ne vel falsa legat taceat vel forte repente
Ante pios fratres lector in ecclesia.[1]

This caution may be directed against idle chatter; but muttering and whispering would be equally objectionable. Dictation was probably but little employed in monasteries as a means of multiplying copies of manuscripts,[2] and where not more than one copy at a time was expected, silence was the rule. At Tournai in the twelfth century, the Abbé Odo had books copied, 'ita ut si claustrum ingredereris, videres plerumque xii monachos juvenes in cathedris sedentes et super tabulas diligenter et artificiose compositas cum silentio scribentes'.[3] The arrangement of certain monastic libraries suggests the same purpose. Part of the cloister was often used for reading and perhaps writing, and was divided into niches or stalls, each to contain a monk and his book. In the Rites of Durham (Surtees Society, vol. CVII (1902), p. 83) a description of this arrangement is given: 'in the north syde of the Cloister from the corner over against the Church Dour to the corner over againste the Dorter dour was all fynely glased from the hight to the sole within a litle of the grownd into the Cloyster garth, and in every wyndowe iii pewes or Carrells where every one of the old monkes had his Carrell severall by himselfe, that when they had dyned they dyd resorte to that place of Cloister, and there studyed upon there bookes, every one in his

1 Dümmler, *Poetae Lat. aevi Carol.* I, p. 320, quoted by Louis Havet, *Manuel de Critique verbale*, Paris, 1911, p. 125.

2 Apparently, dictation was employed chiefly in legal and notarial circles but mistakes occur in literary texts which can hardly be explained as due to 'self-dictation' induced by the acoustic habits of the scribe. In *Girart de Roussillon*, ed. E. B. Ham, Yale, 1939, l. 1858, *estouvoir* appears in one MS. as *es tout voir*. In *La Grant Ystoire de Monsignor Tristan 'li Bret'*, ed. F. C. Johnson, London, 1942, p. 11, *je n'arai, amins*, is given as *naramins* by the Edinburgh MS. In Peirol, *Pus flum Jordan ai vist*, stanza 3, the reading *qu'en la terra a croy emendamen*, can be certainly corrected to *qu'Englaterra*. Mistakes of this kind are familiar to anyone who has to correct school copies from dictation. An instance occurs in *Les Discours du Docteur O'Grady* (p. 49), where M. Maurois refers to the regimental padre as 'le vieil homme'; what he misheard was 'the 'oly man'.

3 Havet, p. 253; Lindsay, *Introduction to Latin Textual Emendation*, p. 75.

Carrell all the after none unto evensong tyme; this was there Exercise every daie; all there pewes or Carrells was all fynely wainscotted, and verie close all but the fore part which had carved wourke that gave light in at ther carrell doures of wainscott; and in every Carrell was a deske to lye there bookes on; and the Carrells was no greater then from one stanchell of the wyndowe to another'. A similar arrangement was in force in the cloister of Gloucester Abbey. Why this attempt to secure privacy in establishments where the inmates as a rule spent most of their time among their fellows? For the same reason that the reading-room of the British Museum is not divided into sound-proof compartments. The habit of silent reading has made such an arrangement unnecessary; but fill the reading-room with medieval readers and the buzz of whispering and muttering would be intolerable.

These facts deserve greater attention from the editors of medieval texts. When the eye of a modern copyist leaves the manuscript before him in order to write, he carries in his mind a visual reminiscence of what he has seen. What the medieval scribe carried was an auditory memory, and probably in many cases, a memory of one word at a time. Zauner[1] has suggested that this habit has had an influence upon the development of final consonants: 'man wird wohl in Afrz. gesprochen haben: *il est arrivez*, aber, *il es morz* (wie etwa *aestimare* nicht *estmer*, sondern *esmer* geworden war), *tot arme*, aber *to muet*. Dass die Schrift davon so gut wie nichts weiss, erklärt sich wohl dadurch, dass die mittelalterlichen Schreiber während des Schreibens die Wörter vor sich hinflüsterten, also wirklich isoliert sprachen.' To this cause may be attributed some of the inconsistencies in the orthography of scribes, which were not necessarily due to mere carelessness; if a scribe was copying a text composed in a dialect not native to himself, he was likely to substitute his own auditory memory of the text for his visual impression of it, and to write *er* instead of *ar*, *el* for *al* and the like. Mistakes may be due to this cause, a case of which occurs in *L'Hystore Job*. This work is a French translation of the Latin *Compendium* made by Peter of Blois (to the order of King Henry II of England) from the *Moralia* completed by Pope Gregory the Great in 590. The translator was a Northerner who wrote in the Picard dialect; the manuscript which has come down to us was probably not copied from the archetype, but

1 *Leuvensche Bijdragen XV*, 1923, III, pp. 77 ff.

from a copy thereof in certain respects defective. The copyist was also a Northerner; his orthography was inconsistent and the editor considers him to have been 'quelquefois plus attentif à sa calligraphie qu'au sens de son modèle' (introd. p. xiv). In vv. 697–701 of the poem he produced an anacoluthon by writing *et* three times instead of *est*. The editor's explanation illustrates the point of this chapter: 'Il reste à expliquer pourquoi le scribe a écrit *et* pour *est* aux vers 697, 698, et 701. Nous croyons être en présence d'un phénomène qui expliquerait mainte faute "orale" de copie dans les manuscrits et qui, du point de vue psychologique, est des plus vraisemblables: le scribe, *en copiant, se prononçait à lui-même* [editor's italics] les mots et ainsi, en quelque sorte, écrivait comme si quelqu'un les lui dictait, en effet; il voyait *est*, il entendait le son approximatif d'*e* fermé, il écrivait *et*, les deux mots ayant, à cette époque, très probablement le même son. A cet endroit, un tel fait est rendu plus probable par l'état même du texte, car la phrase qu'il copiait est si peu claire qu'un scribe qui n'aurait pas l'original latin sous les yeux n'y verrait peut-être qu'une série de phrases prépositionnelles toutes d'une même portée.…' There are other discrepancies in this scribe's orthography which might be explained upon the same principle. Instances can be found elsewhere without difficulty; Paul Meyer's remarks upon the scribe of the unique manuscript of *Guillaume le Maréchal* (*Société de l'Histoire de France*, Paris, 1891, III, pp. cxxxvi ff.) show that he was an Englishman imposing his own orthography upon a French original which he was copying, and several of his deformations of place and proper names with which he was not familiar are due to his reliance upon auditory memory.

To the same tendency may be due the rimes in Beroul's *Tristran* (ed. A. Ewert, Blackwell, 1940), *vóier* : *soir*, l. 473; *choier* : *doloir*, l. 3937, where the scribe has substituted his own pronunciation for the correct rime in -*oir*. It must also be remembered that the individual cannot criticise the correctness of his own pronunciation; mimetic capacity varies greatly in individuals and the speaker is himself no judge of his success or failure in imitating the sounds he hears. A German immigrant to America will pronounce 'dollar' as 'dahler' on the analogy of 'thaler', and remain sublimely unconscious that his pronunciation is incorrect; he identifies a mistaken auditory memory of the word with a correct visual memory of it. It is also possible for the two memories to become confused, when a word will be spelt differently, even when it recurs in close succession; in *La Chastelaine de Saint-Gille* (ed. Schultz-Gora, Halle, 1899), ll. 252 ff., we have

> La sainte croiz d'outre mer
> ...nous soit hui en *aie*!
> En *aide* nous puist hui estre
> La sainte croiz.

In *Doon de la Roche* (A.T.F. 1921), ll. 1631 ff.:

> 'Cil Damedex de gloire qui en crois fu penez,
> Il *saut* icest borjois et lui et son barné.'
> Quant l'entendit li ostes, si a le chef levé:
> 'Seignor, et Dieus vos *salve*!' dist Gontiaumes li ber.

So Anglo-Norman writers rime *Deus* : *tels*, vocalising the *l* in the latter word, without concern for consistency of orthography, for which their visual memory was weak. In *Orson de Beauvais* (A.T.F. 1899, composed 1180–85, ed. Gaston Paris) the rimes show that the author's French was Francien-Picard. The scribe was from Lorraine, and introduced forms from his own dialect without any kind of system, the result being, in the words of the editor, 'un mélange incohérent'. He wrote *a* for *ai*, *avra* for *avrai*, and inversely, *ai* for *a*, *alait* for *alat*, *pourais* for *pouras*. Initial *es* he changed to *a*, *acouter* for *escouter*, *amolu* for *esmolu*; inversely, again, he used *es* for *a*, *esdoubler* for *adouber*, *espotre* for *apotre*. He was a mechanical and careless copyist, who often misunderstood the text and omitted single lincs and even whole passages; sometimes he retained a visual impression of the text before him, but he was more inclined to trust his auditory memory; he wrote, for instance, *estargier* three times, but *atarjant* once.

Instances in which the difference between auditory and visual memory can be made a basis for emendation will naturally vary in frequency with the education and competence of the scribe. On the whole, the orthography of French texts in the twelfth and thirteenth centuries is surprisingly uniform and suggests an elaboration of rules and a training of scribes more extensive than might have been expected at so early a period. But training and experience varied in different cases. Editors of texts have to estimate the competence of any scribe with whose work they have to deal; such cases cannot be subjected to fixed rules and scribes have to be considered as individuals, and it is no waste of time to consider the psychological reasons for their mistakes and aberrations.

CHAPTER III

LANGUAGE & NATIONALITY

MEDIEVAL and modern times are in striking contrast in their attitude towards language, regarded as a mark of nationality. Nothing could be less medieval than the exhortation of the schoolmaster, M. Hamel, in Daudet's *conte*, *La Dernière Classe*, delivered when German was to become the official and compulsory language of Alsace-Lorraine: 'il se mit à nous parler de la langue française, disant que c'était la plus belle langue du monde, la plus claire, la plus solide; qu'il fallait la garder entre nous et ne jamais l'oublier, parce que, quand un peuple tombe esclave, tant qu'il tient bien sa langue, c'est comme s'il tenait la clef de sa prison'. Language had little or no political significance in the middle ages. No ruler dreamt of attempting to suppress one language in order to impose another upon a conquered race. Such prohibitions as have affected Poland, Alsace-Lorraine, Czecho-Slovakia, Tirol, in the immediate past, are modern innovations. Rome never regarded language as a bone of political contention. Under the Roman Empire the use and spread of Greek was unrestricted. Cicero could address the Syracusan senate in Greek; Greek inscriptions of the seventh century A.D. have been found as near to Rome as Naples, and the debt of Christianity to the κοινή, the vernacular of the Levant, is beyond calculation. Of other languages it may be said, *in Tiberim defluxit Orontes*, without let or hindrance. Nor did the Romans make any attempt to impose their Latin upon subject races by the suppression of vernacular tongues. Celtic and Iberian died out and were supplanted by Latin in Gaul and Spain, not only because Latin was the official and legal language, but also because it was the language of a higher and more attractive civilisation.[1] Spanish tribesmen were eager to be latinised;

---

1 Roman insistence upon Latin as the official language was naturally strict. Tiberius (Suetonius, chap. 71) insisted upon its use as the army language; Claudius dismissed a Greek official for breaking this rule (Suetonius, chap. 71). The passage in St Augustine (*De Civitate Dei*, XIX, chap. 7): 'Opera data est ut imperiosa civitas non solum jugum, verum etiam linguam suam domitis gentibus per pacem sociatis imperaret', does not imply any attempt to suppress vernacular tongues.

Sertorius organised a Latin school for young nobles at Huesca about 80 B.C., and the long list of eminent writers and administrators of Spanish and Celtic extraction which succeeding centuries can show is sufficient evidence of the readiness with which these peoples accepted Roman culture. In the middle ages, the sense of universalism, the acceptance of the Empire, of the Catholic Church and of Latin as its official language outweighed any sense of national feeling that might have inspired respect for a vernacular. Walther von der Vogelweide thinks of the Empire as a political, not as a linguistic unity.

There was the further general feeling that the end of all things was at hand, that life here was unimportant in comparison with the life to come, and the idea of progress, in our sense of the term, was hardly apprehended. Hence the great amount of didactic literature that these ages produced and the idea that language was, like other matters, only a temporary arrangement. The chief concern of those who thought and wrote was to use a medium that would enable them to communicate their meaning to others. For theological, or what may be called scientific purposes, Latin naturally came first; it was generally known, and it possessed the vocabulary required for dealing with technical subjects, to a degree which no vernacular could claim. Writers upon subjects of more popular interest were ready to abandon the language of their infancy for a foreign tongue at the call of cultural or aesthetic considerations. Brunetto Latini, in the thirteenth century, wrote his *Trésor* in French for the reason that in his opinion 'La parleure française est plus delitable et plus commune à toutes gens'; a similar reason for the same procedure is given by the chronicler Martino da Canale: 'La langue française cort parmi le monde et est plus delitable à lire et à oïr que nule autre.' The Catalan troubadour, Ramon Vidal de Besalù, who lived probably at the end of the twelfth century, explains in his preface to his *Rasos de Trobar* that he writes to show what language is correct for lyric poetry and states that 'la parladura francesca val mais et es plus avinens a far romanz, retronsas et pasturellas, mas cella de Lemosin val mais per far vers et cansos et serventes'. The distinction was due to a convention which laid down that the choice of language was determined by the literary *genre* in question and not by the nationality of the author. A parallel case is provided by the so-called Franco-Italian literature which appeared from the thirteenth to the fifteenth century. Apart from such writers as Brunetto Latini, Martino da Canale, Philip of

Novara, the editor of Marco Polo's travels, who had an adequate command of French, there were a number of others who wrote a hybrid language which was neither French nor Italian; of these, two classes are distinguished. There were writers who remodelled French *chansons de geste*, whose style shows clear traces of Italian dialect, traces of a nature that cannot be attributed to copyists; Italian words and expressions are used which are unknown to French; grammatical forms are influenced by Italian phonetics; prosody is often as much Italian as French. These influences were not sufficiently strong in the better class of writers to obscure the French element; but a lower class produced a wholly barbarous jargon in which French and Northern Italian dialect are completely confused. They were not merely remodelling French originals, but writing compositions of their own in the style of the *chanson de geste*, for which reason they preferred to write in what they thought was French, the language assigned by convention to that particular literary *genre*. These differences were individual and were due to different degrees of culture and education; lyric poetry in Northern Italy of the thirteenth century was written in Provençal, and the writers were cultured court poets whose compositions rarely show Italianisms; writers of narrative poetry belonged to a lower class of society and were not greatly concerned to consider refinements of language.[1]

Similarly, in Spain, literary convention decreed that Alfonso X, a Castilian, should write his *Cantigas* in the thirteenth century in the Galician dialect, which was regarded as the proper medium for lyric poetry. Choice of language might, of course, be decided by personal preference or dislike; German was compared by some troubadours with the croaking of frogs or the barking of dogs; they were probably predisposed by a dislike of German manners to condemn the sound of a language which they did not understand:

> Alamans trob deschauzutz e vilans;
> E quand negus si feing esser cortes,
> Ira mortals cozens et enois es:
> E lor parlars sembla lairar de cans.[2]

1 For examples and references to literature on the subject, see G. Bertoni, *Il Duecento* (Storia Letteraria d' Italia), Milano ,1930, cap. IV, and p. 125 below.

2 Peire Vidal, ed. Anglade (*Classiques français du moyen âge*, p. 116). The troubadour references to Germans have been collected by Crescini in an article, *Broder, Guaz!* contributed to a *Miscellany presented to L. E. Kastner*, Cambridge, 1932, p. 147.

'I regard Germans as mean and low; and when one of them makes a pretence of courtesy, it is mortal grief and burning annoyance: their speech resembles the barking of dogs.'

At a much later date, Margaret of Navarre declared (*Heptameron*, no. 24) 'le langage castillan est sans comparaison mieux déclarant cette passion d'amour que n'est le françois'.

Writers who abandoned their mother tongue in order to write in German are not common. Probably the best known case is that of Thomasin von Zerclaere, who states that he was born in Friuli; he was a canon of Aquileia, a member of the local noble family of the Cerchiari (whence his name), and died before 1238. His work, *Der Welsche Gast*, is the first Middle High German didactic work of importance; by the term *welsch* he means Italian or foreign, and personifies himself in the title of the work as the 'foreign guest' who comes to teach strangers as a stranger. This point he makes plain at the outset of his poem (l. 33): 'Here I would have you know that, well as I can speak a foreign tongue, I do not wish to mix foreign words with my composition. Moral teaching demands for itself a simple dress, and I do not deny that anyone who colours his German with foreign terms displeases me. When a German who has no knowledge of another tongue goes to the book for instruction, he will be troubled by wonderful words, whatever his readiness to learn. I fear that if I attempted to teach you to speak another language, my labour would be wasted. I have another purpose before me which I will industriously pursue and constantly keep in mind, that I may be clearly understood; to that end I will ever strive. Hence you must not be critical, if I should happen to make a false rime (ob mir lîhte geschiht / etlîchen rîm ze überheben / daz er nien werde reht gegeben). The fact that I am not conversant with the language must cause me much anxiety. Therefore I ask all the young, and also beg the learned to do, as they surely will do, out of their knowledge, sense and kindliness, namely, to let pass without criticism whatever defects may appear in my speech. It will be no surprise if I should mispronounce German, seeing that I am a complete foreigner.' Thomasin exaggerated his weakness; critics find few traces of foreign idiom in his German, and his divergences from the normal may be due to the fact that he learnt the language in the Austrian district near his birthplace. His self-depreciation may be classed with the 'captationes benevolentiae' with which German writers often began their works. French poets were more ready to assure their audiences that they were about to hear something new and unusual, extracted from ancient records, known to the poet alone, which they would be well advised not to miss. German writers more frequently ask for indulgence on the ground of their lack of learning, want of style or presumption in venturing to put themselves forward.[1] Quantum mutati!

The difficulty of intercourse between different nationalities raised by difference of language is sometimes recognised and sometimes disregarded by the *chansons de geste*; inconsistency upon this and other matters is to be expected from authors who deal with an imaginary world of fantastic history and wild geography. In *Aliscans*[2] (l. 8327) 'langage' is used as equivalent to 'nation':

> Car Desramés a ja la mer passee,
> De .xx. langages a la gent assamblee.

But in this and other *chansons* strangers appear upon the scene from distant lands and explain their business without any need of an interpreter; Christian knights and Saracen chiefs hurl defiance at one another on the battlefield with complete understanding. In *Les Enfances Guillaume* (ll. 2944 ff., A.T.F. 1935), Guillaume 'fierement appelle' the Saracen Thiebaut:

> Di moi, paiens, per la loi de ta geste,
> Com as tu non, di moi, et de kel terre?

After a contumelious conversation ('Tu ailles a diables', etc.):

> Di moi, vassalz, dist Thiebaus li Escler,
> Per cele loi ke tu ais a garder,
> Coment as non et de kel gent iez neiz?

The reply occupies twelve lines and it is assumed that the interlocutors fully understand one another; examples of this kind could easily be multiplied. On the other hand, in particular cases, the importance of linguistic difference is recognised. In *Florence de Rome* (ll. 1014 ff., A.T.F. 1907) a spy reports to the emperor the plans of the Greeks besieging Rome:

> Ilec ot une espie, que de Rome fu nez,
> A guise de Grifon vestuz et conraez;
> Bien entent le langage, bien en fu doctrinez.

1 See *Die Demutsformel Mittelhochdeutscher Dichter*, von J. Schwietering, Berlin, 1921 (Abhandlungen der Königlichen Gesellschaft der Wissenschaften zu Göttingen), p. 48.   2 Ed. Wienbeck, Hartnacke, Rasch, Hall, 1903.

But the Roman and Byzantine emperors are able to insult one another on the subsequent battlefield with complete mutual understanding. The value of a knowledge of languages as a means of deceiving an enemy is well recognised. In *La Chevalerie Vivien* (l. 863, ed. A. Terracher, 1909), Girart offers to go through the Saracen lines to fetch help:

> Dist Gerars: Sire, g'irai, se vos voles.
> Je sai parler Sarrainois asses;
> Se puis passer les loges et les tres,
> S'il me velt croire, lou secors averes.

(*Il* refers to Guillaume d'Orange.) Similarly, in *Aliscans* (l. 1376), Guillaume, disguised in the armour of an enemy, hopes that his knowledge of languages will enable him to reach Orange undetected:

> Grigois parole, bien en fu latimés,
> Sarrasinois resavoit il assés;
> De tos langages estoit endoctrinés.

Difference of language as an obstacle is occasionally suggested, as in *Galeran de Bretaigne* (l. 5590, *Les Classiques Français du Moyen Age*, L. Foulet, Paris, 1925):

> Alemans y a a plenté,
> Et Avaloys et Brebenchons.
> Entr' eulx demeinent grans tenchons
> Et grant orgueil en leur langaige.

Wace, in the *Roman de Rou* (l. 8254, ed. Andresen, Heilbronn, 1877), says that the Normans were unable to understand the taunts of the English before the Battle of Hastings:

> Cil escutoent e suffreient,
> ne saveient que il diseient;
> co lur ert vis qu'il glatisseient,
> kar lur langage n'entendeient.

In the thirteenth century *Roman de Balain*, the hero and his companion observe that language changes as they travel farther into the country: 'Ensi chevauchierent entre eus deus de jour en jour tant que moult orent eslongié la chité de Camalaoth, et li langages lour commencha si durement a changier qu'il n'entendirent mais se moult petit non.'[1]

---

[1] Manchester University Press, 1942, ed. M. Dominica Legge, p. 70.

Respect for language as a mark of nationality is thus not always pronounced in the *chansons de geste*, unless special circumstances draw attention to differences of language. In *Doon de la Roche* one Malprin is sent on a message, his qualification being, 'bien sot xxx langaiges' (l. 4242), and as he had to travel from Constantinople to France, he probably needed some of them. In *Fouke Fitzwarin*,[1] when he lands with his followers on the Orkneys, 'atant virent un juvencel gardant berbis; e quant vist les chevalers, s'en ala vers eux e les salua de un latyn corumpus'. Later in the narrative, one John de Rampayne, disguised as a merchant, goes to discover the whereabouts of King John: 'e quanqu'il parla fust latyn corupt; mes le meir le entendy bien. Le meir le amena devant le roy Johan a Westmoster, e le marchant mout cortoisement ly salua en son langage. Le roi l'entendi bien.' The 'corrupt Latin' was no doubt a *lingua franca* current in mercantile and maritime districts, and owing its origin, as do similar jargons in modern times, to the necessities of trade. In *Aymeri de Narbonne* (date 1200–25, ed. L. Demaison, A.T.F. 1887) we read of a deputation to Pavia, composed of persons who 'tuit sont sage et bien enlatimé' (l. 1600); they meet the hostile Germans who shout 'comme gent desfaée, Godehelepe' (l. 1635, and 'Godeherre' l. 1734). The German leader, Savari, 'parla romanz, que la terre ot usée' and is able to challenge the French in their own language. 'Enlatimé' is a term apparently confined to Romance languages, so far as this poem is concerned. No language difficulty is mentioned in the negotiations at Pavia, and Aymeri, in the final encounter with the Saracens, is able to defy them in his own language and to be understood.

These linguistic difficulties led to the rise of the professional interpreter, the *latinier* or *latimier* (whence the English family name, Latimer). The term *latin* lost its restricted meaning and was used to denote any kind of language, even the twittering of birds; Latin was known as *grammaire*. A female interpreter is thus described (*Aiol et Mirabel*, l. 5420, ed. Förster, Heilbronn, 1876):

> Ele fu enparlee de xiiii latins,
> Ele sauoit parler et grigois et hermin, (Armenian)
> Flamenc et borgengon et tout le sarrasin,
> Poiteuin et gascon, se li uient a plaisir.

1 Ed. L. Brandin, *Les Classiques français du moyen âge*, Paris, 1930, pp. 60 and 78. (Text of fourteenth century.)

In *Horn*, l. 1351 (ed. Brede and Stengel, Marburg, 1883), we are informed:

> Latimiers ont od els pur mustrer lor curage
> Ki de plusurs latins sunt escolez et sage.

The profession was equally recognised in the South of France, and is mentioned several times in the poem on the Albigeois crusade. The troubadour At de Mons, in one of his moral discourses (II, 573), says:

> Homs pot, segon mo sen,
> Per art o per uzatje
> Entendre tot lengatje,
> Mas non say latinier
> Qu'entenda messongier.

'A man, in my opinion, by skill or use, can understand any language, but I know no interpreter who can understand a liar.'

In the *roman Guilhem de la Barra* (ed. P. Meyer, A.T.F. 1895), a 'Sarrazis latiniers' helps certain arrivals out of their linguistic difficulty and then goes off to report to his master:

> Ab tant lo latiniers s'en va
> Vas so senhor lay hon lo vic,
> E parlan son algavaric
> Tot lo negoci li mostrec.

The term *algavaric*, 'jargon', recalls the fact that, in Spain, Christians who could speak the Moorish language were known as 'algaraviados'. The Moor who could speak Spanish was known as *latinado*, one in command of a Romance language or languages; so, in the *Poema del Cid*, l. 2666:

> Quando esta falssedad dizien los de Carrion,
> Un moro latinado bien gelo entendio.[1]

While differences of language were thus recognised as marking differences of nationality, there is little evidence to show that a language was ever regarded, as it often is to-day, as embodying the soul of a people and therefore as a possession for which men are ready to fight and die. For instance, the rapid decay of troubadour poetry and of

---

[1] James I of Aragon found some difficulty in communicating with the 'Saracens' in his conquest of Mallorca. In the first part of his chronicle, composed after 1230, he speaks of 'un serrahí qui sabia nostre lati' (chap. 86) and of 'un juheu que nos los haviem lliurat per torcimany' (chap. 119).

Provençal literature after the conclusion of the Albigensian wars has occasioned some surprise and some far-fetched explanations. The simple fact is, that there was no sense of nationalism in Southern France sufficiently strong to resist the pressure of Northern French culture, and certainly no general belief that a Southern French dialect was a token of individual nationality. 'Ce n'est que de nos jours qu'on voit des nations privées de leur indépendance s'attacher à maintenir la pureté de leur idiome et la perpétuité de leur littérature. Aussi, pourrait-on dire que, malgré les siècles écoulés depuis l'annexion des pays de langue d'oc à la France, la formation et l'expansion d'une littérature originale dans les provinces du Midi ont plus de chances de réussite aujourd'hui qu'au XIVe siècle.'[1]

The state of affairs in England from the eleventh to the thirteenth century is instructive. While the number of Normans who came and settled in England has been variously estimated and often exaggerated, there is no doubt that Norman French was the official language of the country for some two centuries.

> Li reis amat mult ses Normans;
> Les Engleis enueia as chans.

There is no evidence of any attempt to suppress the English vernacular and to impose French upon the population. The simple fact that all the business of church and state and all intercourse among the governing classes was conducted in French was enough to drive English underground and confine it to the proletariat. French had the same prospects of extension that Latin had enjoyed in Gaul and Spain. But English retained its vitality and the national movement against Henry III and his favouritism of foreigners brought about a rapid revival of the language and stopped the constant influx of foreign contingents. Before this time, Englishmen wrote in French because they considered that they would thus secure a larger public for their works; Walter Map in 1209 criticises Giraldus Cambrensis for not writing in French and so appealing to a wider range of readers and hearers; Peter of Peckham writes in French for the same reason, though he was an Englishman and admits his imperfect mastery of French. Robert of Gretham, an Englishman, writing about 1250, apologises for his defective French and sug-

---

1 P. Meyer, *Les derniers troubadours de la Provence*, Paris, 1871, p. 4. The partial success of the Félibrige movement is confirmation of this view.

gests that the sense is much more important than accuracy or purity of language.

> Si rien i ad a amender
> U del fraunceis u del rimer.
> Nel tenes pas a mesprisoun
> Mes bien gardez la raisoun.

Similar quotations could be produced,[1] covering the period until the early years of the fifteenth century, by which time English was re-established as the dominant language; for instance, Henry of Lancaster, a noble whose French was defective, concludes his *Livre de Seyntz Medecines*[2] in 1354, by apologising: 'si le franceis ne soit pas bon, je doie estre escusee, pur ce que jeo sui engleis et n'ai pas moelt hauntee le franceis'. Writer after writer recognises that Anglo-Norman is a debased idiom, and that his own knowledge of it is imperfect. Why then was the use of it continued? Firstly, because local dialects of English were unintelligible to natives of different localities. William of Malmesbury, writing in the twelfth century, observes, 'sane tota lingua Nordanimbrorum, sed maxime in Eboraco, ita inconditum stridet, ut nichil nos australes intelligere possimus'.[3] French had made its way into the country districts by the end of the thirteenth century to such an extent that many people could understand it, even if they could not speak it, and works written to be read aloud had, therefore, some chance of a hearing.[4] At the end of the fifteenth century Caxton found, when he began printing, that what was understood in one part of England might prove to be difficult or even unintelligible in another part. As Chaucer noted:

> And for ther is so gret diversite
> In Englissh and in writyng of oure tonge,
> So prey I God that non myswrite the,
> Ne the mysmetre for defaute of tonge.
> And red wherso thow be, or elles songe
> That thow be understonde, God I beseche!

1 Some are given by Vising, *Anglo-Norman Language and Literature*, Oxford, 1923, p. 26.
2 Ed. E. J. Arnould for the Anglo-Norman Texts Society, 1940, Blackwell, Oxford, p. 239.
3 *De gestis pontificum*, Rolls Series, 1870, pp. 209, 285.
4 On this point, see the introduction to *Les Contes Moralisés de Bozon* (A.T.F. 1889, pp. li ff.).

If such was the difficulty in Chaucer's time, it is obvious that at an earlier date a writer in English could hope for little more than a very local reputation.[1] Secondly, French was the fashionable language; ignorance of it argued a lack of culture and English was despised as a patois. Thus it is laid down by the statutes of the General Chapter of the Province of York, on 23 September 1290:[2] 'Et quia videtur utile et hónestum, qui se garritui Anglico assuescunt et ad magnates sepius pro domus sue negociis diriguntur, ne pro defectu boni ydiomatis incidant in ruborem, statutum est ut omnes in capitulo, in proclamationibus, correcionibus, colloquiis, parlamentis, solaciis ac locis aliis colloquantur Gallicum seu Latinum; qui autem secus fuerit, in capitulo publice proclametur, et secundum meritum puniatur.'

If for these reasons writers who had an inadequate command of French felt obliged to use the language, why did they not make some effort to correct their deficiencies? An Englishman who writes in a foreign language under similar conditions secures the services of a native to read his work for the purpose of removing Anglicisms and correcting inaccuracies. The English writer of the eleventh or twelfth century probably felt no necessity for such a precaution. His work was to be read aloud, and the majority of his solecisms and false concords would pass unnoticed. Such apologies as an author made for his defective knowledge of French were intended to conciliate the very few who might read his works. There was no army of reviewers to scarify his defects in periodical publications. There was, moreover, no body of public opinion agreed upon the necessity of accurate scholarship when a vernacular was in question. Even in the case of Latin, there were some pre-Carolingians who had objected to the tyranny of grammar and syntax; Gregory of Tours[3] says: 'Veniam legentibus precor si aut in litteris aut in sillabis grammaticam artem excessero, de qua adplene non sum imbutus.' Gregory the Great declared: 'I do not shun at all the confusion of barbarians. I despise the proper constructions and cases, because I think it very unfitting that the words of the celestial oracle should be restricted by the rules of Donatus.' Charlemagne's educational reforms and the revival of learning in the year 1000 did something to remove this attitude

1 Essays and Studies by members of the English Association, vol. XXIII, 1938: *The Author and his Public*, by H. S. Bennett.
2 Camden Society, *Third Series*, XLV, p. 260.
3 Quoted by Vising, p. 27.

of indifference to scholarship; but the large amount of evidence collected by Dr Coulton[1] suggests that sound Latinists were not numerous and that the Church which was concerned to maintain the supremacy of Latin as the language of piety and learning could provide abundant examples of every kind of ignorance. From the twelfth century onwards we find a succession of ecclesiastics and chroniclers who wrote correct Latin in a style which indicates habitual use of the language; but it was an artificial language maintained for communication with foreigners, for doctrinal reasons and for business purposes; an increasing tendency to use a vernacular is steadily perceptible. But Latinists who had been brought up on Donatus and Priscian, if they had really learned their lesson, would know the difference between good Latin and bad; they would have in their minds a definite linguistic ideal. Grammar and syntax had been codified and supported by examples drawn from works consecrated by the admiration of centuries.

Did this training suggest to them that a vernacular might also be thus treated and might become a field for scholarship? The most that can be said is that Latin was regarded as a stable language, whereas change in the case of vernaculars was taken for granted; dialectical differences delayed linguistic uniformity until the fourteenth century, when grammars, vocabularies and phrase-books began to appear. In England, for instance, dialect was especially marked. William of Malmesbury's reference to the Northumbrians, quoted above, is repeated in Higden's *Polychronicon*. Until some one dialect had secured recognition as the standard language of society, attempts to codify usage or to produce grammars were hopeless. Where French was concerned, it was always possible to refer to France for a criterion; thus Walter Map can satirise the French of Marlborough, as Chaucer at a later date poked fun at the French of Stratford atte Bowe. On the other hand, there are indications that the manner of speech was regarded as evidence of social standing and culture. Jocelyn of Brakelonde says of Abbot Samson: 'Homo erat eloquens, Gallice et Latine... Scripturam Anglice scriptam legere novit elegantissime, et Anglice sermocinari solebat populo, sed secundum linguam Norfolchie, ubi natus et nutritus erat.'[2] Here a contrast is made between English and the dialect of Norfolk; 'legere', as often, means to read aloud, and the Abbot's diction when reading from a text seems

1 *Europe's Apprenticeship*, London, 1940.
2 Ed. J. G. Rokewode, Camden Society, London, 1840, p. 30.

to be contrasted with the ruder English in which he addressed his own people. In *Joufrois*[1] (l. 2203):

> Apres mangier a l'avespree
> Entra par la sale pavee....
> Uns serjanz....
> Beaus fu et apert et corteis
> Et si sot bien parler Franceis;

in other words, he spoke better than the servant class, a hint that he was in disguise. The novel of Raimon Vidal, *Abrils issi* (l. 1625), describing one character, says:

> E de vilan parler estret,

and thus makes a distinction between cultivated and common speech.

Class distinctions of various kinds are inevitable in any population and speech is constantly regarded as a distinguishing sign of culture or the lack of it. This is but the beginning of a process which may end in the domination of one or other mode of speech, provided that political and social currents happen to set in its favour. But until the written becomes the printed word and education enables a wide public to read for themselves, instead of depending upon recitation, linguistic stability is hardly possible. The written or printed language professes to represent the standard tongue; from this the spoken language tends continually to diverge, through its readiness to follow individual innovations which become fashionable. The bulwark of resistance to these is the printed language, which is modified only when new forms have become so widespread that they cannot be ignored. When this stage has been reached, when literature and history are circulated in forms accessible to the public, and when some interest in the country's past has been aroused, the basis has been laid for the formation of a national linguistic consciousness, and a language is felt to be the expression of tribal or racial characteristics. For print alone can secure the indispensable conditions of standardisation, the substitution of visual for acoustic word-memory. Not until an educated public begins to respect the printed word and to resent aberration from it, does scholarship and respect for verbal accuracy come to be regarded as a moral duty. Some progress in this direction was certainly made before the invention of printing.

1 Ed. K. Hofmann and F. Muncker, Halle, 1880.

The orthography of French texts in the twelfth and thirteenth centuries is, as has been said, surprisingly uniform and suggests that some codification of scribal habits and customs had been secured between different *scriptoria*; even so, as in the orthography of Mr Weller's name, much might depend upon 'the taste and fancy of the speller'; and a visual word-memory is not so readily developed by the use of written as of printed texts.

This is not to assert that the domination of print did not involve certain disadvantages. Script and, to a far greater extent, print follow and do not anticipate the development of the spoken language; they preserve archaisms and are chary of admitting neologisms; they help the development of a literary language and style which is often far removed from current habits of speech; the accusation of 'talking like a book' (and, perhaps, of not shutting up so easily) would otherwise be pointless. Even worse is the fact that print and script, as developments from an unscientific age, have rarely succeeded in giving a true phonetic transcription of the sounds which they profess to represent: this initial difficulty is increased by the conservatism of readers and writers, who resent change in what is to them familiar. School instruction starts with the book, and the book's orthography is regarded as a kind of legal code against which there is no appeal. Meanwhile, language develops, and sounds change, but 'spelling' remains fixed, unless the tinkering of amateur philologists helps to make confusion worse confounded, with the result that English orthography is now the despair of Europe, while that of France leaves much to be desired. The fundamental reason for divergence between the spoken and written language is the fact that a visual image is more lasting and more readily appropriated than an acoustic image; when speech and orthography fail to agree, script or print usually gain the upper hand; only the phonetician and the philologist can settle such disputes, and in the improbable event that their advice is requested, it is not likely to be followed; society finds great comfort in 'leaving well alone'.[1]

Thus England never had a 'standard' Anglo-Norman language. Until the middle of the thirteenth century, when a national movement began with the antagonism to foreign immigrants consequent upon the loss of the French provinces and the misgovernment of the crown,

1 See L. Foulet, *La Disparition du Prétérit*, in *Romania*, XLVI (1920), p. 274; De Saussure, *Cours de Linguistique Générale*, Paris, 1923, pp. 45 ff.

Anglo-Norman was a living speech, a dialect of French, subject to the special influences which modified it in a new environment. This modification proceeded rapidly during the twelfth and the early thirteenth centuries, when the language was widely used by a population of mixed or of pure English descent; sounds unfamiliar to the English ear were modified, and the explosive stress accent affected unstressed syllables and diphthongs. The effect of this accent was especially noticeable in verse; the irregularities apparent in Anglo-Norman prosody were caused by an instinctive rejection of the French syllabic system in favour of one that secured the regular repetition of accented syllables, and disregarded, within certain limits, unstressed syllables. In the thirteenth century, divergence had proceeded so far that Anglo-Norman occasionally became a subject of derision upon the continent; and by the end of the century, separation had gone so far, that the language was no longer a mother tongue and was regarded as a subject for school instruction; this was the period when word lists, conversation manuals and grammars were compiled, which, with the exception of the Provençal treatises, were the first attempts in Europe to codify the usage of a vernacular. When Francien became supreme in fourteenth-century France, it was regarded as standard French in England, and those who had occasion to acquire a command of French for diplomatic or other purposes went abroad to learn it. Anglo-Norman had ceased to live.

These conditions were reflected in the disconcerting variations of Anglo-Norman orthography. A scribe might be familiar with Latin, French or English tradition, or possibly with more than one of these; anything like a definite Anglo-Norman tradition was never evolved.[1] Some of the scribal spellings represent pronunciation more effectively than the continental orthography could do; *dekes* for *desque*, *sein* for

1 For details, see M. K. Pope, *From Latin to Modern French*, Manchester, 1934, part v; K. Lambley, *The French Language in England*, Manchester, 1920, chaps. I and II; A. Owen, *Le Traité de Walter de Bibbesworth*, Paris, 1929; L. E. Menger, *The Anglo-Norman Dialect*, London, 1904; F. Brunot, *Histoire de la Langue française*, Paris, 1905, vol. I, pp. 366–74 and chap. v. In a thirteenth-century list of festivals upon which the nuns of Heyham nunnery in Kent were allowed more abundant rations (pittances), we find 'La veile de Pantekuste', and exactly beneath this entry 'Le ior de Pantecuste'. The scribe did not use *c* in the second case from any lack of room for *k*: it was a matter of indifference to him by which symbol he represented the sound concerned. In the Cheltenham Provençal *chansonnier*, *l mouillée* is represented on the same page by *lh, li, ll*. Examples of such inconsistency could easily be multiplied indefinitely.

saint, ver for *veeir* and the like are cases in point. But, and especially in the latter days of the dialect, scribal attempts to represent pronunciation often confuse symbols used to represent any particular sound, with results that resemble the schoolboy effort, *je parlé* for *je parlais*, the effect of auditory as opposed to visual memory; intelligible when read aloud, but offensive to the instructed eye. Thus the Latin *videt* and *vadit* which produced (phonetically) *vęt* in the thirteenth century, appear as *vet, veit, vait, voit, voet, vai, vei, voi*. Compilers of various spelling manuals vainly attempted to reduce this chaos to order; only in the chanceries and in legal circles was any orthographical stability gradually assured, and when this process was complete, Anglo-Norman had been superseded as a medium of common intercourse or of literary composition.

Two instances of medieval movements towards the standardisation of language are of particular interest. It has long been recognised that the lyric poetry of the troubadours shows hardly any trace of dialect, though the poets belonged by birth to districts the dialects of which are clearly marked in local records and also in early literary texts. Poets, whatever their origin, used a common language, a κοινή, intelligible to audiences wherever Provençal was spoken. The development of such a unified language was the inevitable result of an occupation which was carried on by wandering singers, who performed before very different audiences and would naturally be anxious to avoid disturbing their hearers by marked peculiarities of pronunciation or delivery. There is no question in the South of France of attributing to any preponderant political state an influence which made for unification, as was the case in Northern France and in Spain. The South was never politically homogeneous; but the Counts of Toulouse did exert political authority over a considerable district, and a district which included a number of famous courts to which troubadours were glad to resort; here may have been the centre from which a unifying movement began. But this standardised language was not marked by any grammatical exclusiveness; it admitted numerous alternative grammatical forms, as may be seen by turning the pages of the introduction to any Provençal chrestomathy. The intricacy of the rime-schemes employed no doubt inclined poets to liberality and even to license in the admission of variant word-forms to the poetic vocabulary;[1] and orthographical variation was great.

1 For an account of controversy on this point, see Jeanroy, *La Poésie lyrique des Troubadours*, Paris, 1934, I, pp. 45 ff.

This tendency went even further in the case of epic poetry. The jongleur was expected to include *chansons de geste* in his repertoire: if his connection with patrons brought him into areas where Northern and Southern dialects were in transition and were separated by a zone dialectically indeterminate, a certain amount of retouching would make the poem intelligible to any audience: hence the mixture of forms, often inconsistently used, in *Girart de Roussillon, Daurel et Beton* and others. The result of this procedure was an artificial, hybrid language; but the fact that it was understood was sufficient justification for its use.

A similar tendency produced considerable uniformity in the language of the German Minnesänger. Whereas the earlier epic poems were composed in well-marked dialects; the courtly poets of the best period in Middle High German literature developed a poetical language in which dialectical features and grammatical differences were obliterated as far as possible. The Germans were, in short, driven by the nature of their poetic occupation to follow the same course as the Provençal troubadours, in order to make themselves intelligible to audiences far and wide. It does not seem that these conventions were ever codified or that they were very strictly observed. 'Das "klassische" Mittelhochdeutsch ist in der in unsern Grammatiken und in den kritischen Textausgaben fest gesetzten Regelmässigkeit weder gesprochen noch geschrieben worden, diese stellen nur ein sprachliches Idealsystem dar.'[1]

The first attempt to codify prevailing practice was not made by a Provençal but by a Catalan troubadour, Raimon Vidal of Besalù; in a brief treatise, *Las Razos de Trobar*, he defines in terms of geography the meaning of *lengua lemosina*, and studies the several parts of grammar with special reference to morphology. Raimon Vidal insisted that the lack of critical capacity among the numerous lovers of poetry led the poets astray and tended to lower the standard of performance. Some people would pretend to understand a song of which they had comprehended nothing, for fear of being thought stupid; others, who had some critical intelligence, would praise a poor performance from politeness. Raimon's views, intended to establish a standard of criticism, are based upon the usage followed by the best troubadours, though he is prepared to criticise licenses which some of them allowed, and objects to the use of forms current in other dialects more or less related to that

1 G. Ehrismann, *Geschichte der Deutschen Literatur*, zweiter Teil, erste Hälfte, p. 28.

which he termed *lemosi*. He thus recognised a literary language formed by the most famous troubadours in the strongest centre of culture and his attempt is probably the first of its kind. Raimon Vidal lived at the end of the twelfth and the beginning of the thirteenth centuries; the next treatise of importance is the *Donatz Proensals* of Uc Faidit, written in Italy for the benefit of two Italian lords, about 1240. This work exactly follows the method of the famous Latin grammar by Aelius Donatus, the master of St Jerome. Uc Faidit was a pedant with little critical sense; but his persuasion that Latin was the supreme language, to which all others ought to conform, is an idea eminently medieval. He had some trouble in bringing Provençal forms into harmony with Latin grammar; the system of declension, for instance, proved intractable. His purpose was, like that of Raimon Vidal, to standardise the literary language, as may have been inferred from the concluding words of his treatise: 'Ugo nominor, qui librum composui precibus Jacobi de Mora et domini Corani Zhuchii de Sterlleto ad dandam doctrinam vulgaris Provincialis et ad discernendum verum a falso in dicto vulgare.'[1] Both of them have the credit of being the first to recognise that the usages of a vernacular, when it has attained some literary stability, can be codified in 'grammatical' form. As they had probably been brought up on Donatus, they naturally followed his system, and the close imitation of Uc Faidit suggests that he had in view the needs of others who had followed the same course of education.

The next treatise of the kind was the *Leys d'Amors*. When the Consistory of the Gai Savoir was founded at Toulouse in 1323, the chancellor of the consistory, Guilhem Molinier, was commissioned to draw up a code which would guide the judges of the poetical competitions to be

---

1 *Grammaires Provençales*, par F. Guessard, Paris, 1858, p. 65. Information upon these treatises and others is best summarised by Anglade, *Las Leys d'Amors*, Toulouse, 1920, IV, pp. 92 ff. Raimon Feraud, who finished his *Vida de Saint Honorat* in 1300, recognised a standard literary Provençal and regrets his own inability to conform to it:

> 'E si deguns m'asauta
> Mon romanz ni mons ditz,
> Car non los ay escritz
> En lo dreg proensal,
> Non m'o tengan a mal;
> Car ma lenga non es
> Del drech proensales.'

instituted by the consistory, and would also instruct young poets upon questions of language and style. Molinier certainly knew the treatise of Ramon Vidal and was probably acquainted with that of Uc Faidit, which seems never to have obtained much celebrity. Two prose versions of the *Leys* exist, the differences between which do not affect the body of the work, which consists of five parts, treating of orthography and phonetics, metre and prosody, grammar, rhetoric and the figures of rhetoric, and finally general observations both of a literary and moralising character; for the consistory and the company which it represented laid stress upon the religious character of their foundation. For the next two centuries this work exerted a considerable influence in Catalonia and also in Spain; the Marquis of Santillana refers to it in his *Proemio*; Juan Alfonso de Baena alludes to it in the introduction to his *Cancionero*. It does not seem to have been known in Northern France, where the first treatise of the kind, the *Art de Dictier* by Eustache Deschamps, did not appear until 1392.

This attempt to revive the spirit of troubadour poetry was not successful. Poetical competitions conducted by learned academies rarely produce poets; the observance of the 'laws' which governed the character of the compositions led the competitors into pedantry and formalism, and the insistence upon the religious motive as a subject for poetry imposed difficulties upon competitors which only a rare spirit of inspiration could have surmounted. The best troubadour poetry had been produced under conditions of which hardly a vestige remained in the fourteenth century; all that could be done was to preserve as the type of literary language that which was current in the Toulouse area and was regarded as most nearly representing the language of the 'classical' troubadours. This task was accomplished at a time when divergence between Southern French dialects was increasing, and the lead thus given was followed in Catalonia. But linguistic unity cannot be secured by the decrees of academies, even in our days; current usage changes continually, and if there is no such conservative influence as that exerted by print and a public dependent upon print, linguistic change proceeds apace and unregulated, except by the vacillations of fashion. Moreover, Molinier and his company seem to have brought a certain spirit of defeatism to their undertaking; if technical vocabulary was wanting to their own language, they considered that it should be supplied from Latin, 'quar es lengatges mays perfieytz e mays aproatz que

degus dels autres a nos conogutz'. Such words do not suggest the
burning flame of affection for his native tongue with which Dante
entered upon a similar investigation.

There is little doubt that Dante was acquainted with some at least of
these treatises; but he regarded the problem of a vernacular language
from a far wider point of view. The Provençaux were not interested in
the relations between the language or dialects of Northern France and
their own; they were willing to concede that French might, in certain
cases, be a more suitable language than Provençal, as indeed were certain
Italians. The common element in French and Provençal was a subject
beyond their scope. But Dante's ideal comprehended the whole of
Italy and Sicily. His deep love for his own language and his conviction
of its possibilities led him to challenge the supremacy of Latin, and to
stigmatise those who preferred to use other tongues as 'abominable
wretches of Italy who hold cheap that precious vulgar tongue, which,
if it is worthless in any respect, is so only when it is heard from the
meretricious lips of these adulterers' (*Convivio*, I, xi). He certainly
described Latin as noble and sovereign on account of its stability as
compared with a vernacular which is subject to change, and for its
capacity to express abstract ideas in which respect vernaculars are de-
ficient; but a vernacular can also be described as noble and illustrious,
because it is the natural and universal means of communication. When
therefore Dante wrote his *De Vulgari Eloquentia* he was not vindicating
his native tongue against Latin, but against those who scorned it in
favour of other languages. Otherwise, why should he have written his
defence of the vulgar tongue in Latin, after producing so many excellent
reasons for writing the *Convivio* in Italian? His arguments were scientific
and technical, and it was to readers whose education had been based on
Latin that he appealed.[1] He was able to recognise the relationship of the
three Romance languages, but could not account for this by referring
to their derivation from one source. The striking fact for Dante is the
tendency to subdivision which all languages show; all human life is
subject to change, and in the case of language, this process produces
different effects in different localities. Hence men fail to understand one

[1] The controversies that have arisen concerning Dante's theories are discussed in the introduction to A. Marigo's edition of the *De Vulgari Eloquentia*,
Firenze, 1938. See also A. Ewert, *Dante's Theory of Language*, in *M.L.R.* XXXV,
no. 3, p. 355.

another and so 'the inventors of the art of grammar were set in motion; grammar is a kind of unchangeable identity of speech in different localities, times and places. This was settled by the common consent of many peoples, is exposed to the arbitrary will of no particular people and therefore cannot be variable.' Grammar, which is Latin, met the need for a universal language, free from all local or temporal influence which might modify it. It was thus regarded by Dante as a special invention, standing apart from vernaculars, which are not artificial but natural products. The vulgar tongue is our natural speech, which we learn from those about us, as soon as we can speak at all, without the necessity of memorising rules and forms; Latin has to be learnt by study of these, and few members of society are able to acquire command of it.

Dante gave Italian precedence over the other Romance languages because it showed in his opinion a closer resemblance to Latin than did any of them, and because he considered that the best lyric poetry had been composed in Italian. The question then arose, what Italian? Some fourteen principal dialects were enumerated; which of these was to be regarded as the illustrious Italian vulgar tongue? Investigation showed that this tongue is perceptible in varying degrees in all dialects, the evidence being provided by the work of poets who belonged to widely separated districts. The conclusion is, that the illustrious vulgar tongue in Italy 'is that which belongs to all the towns in Italy, but does not appear to belong to any one of them; it is that by which all the local dialects of the Italians are measured, weighed and compared'. To what extent Dante was influenced by theological and scholastic methods of argument in arriving at this conclusion, or to what extent these methods were erroneous need not concern us here. He asserted that there existed a standard Italian which was not the possession of any one town or locality, but the existence of which could be inferred by examining the work of writers who employed it. This language he believed could be further improved and enriched for use as a literary instrument adaptable to the treatment of any kind of subject-matter, *illustre, mediocre* or *humile*.

Here is something new in medieval conceptions of language. Not only is Dante's work the first treatise which can claim the epithet of philological; it is also the first that was written to expound the subject from a national and not a parochial point of view. But to say that Dante discovered language as the symbol of nationality and as a means of uniting politically divided Italians is to exaggerate almost recklessly.

Language was not yet regarded as a political trademark; before the state of 'cujus regio, ejus lingua' could be reached, the stage of 'cujus regio, ejus religio' was to be experienced. The unity of Italy for Dante is geographical and linguistic; his love is 'del bel paese là, dove il *sì* suona'. In Canto VI, l. 76, of the *Purgatorio* there is no hope of political unity:

> Ahi serva Italia, di dolore ostello,
> Nave senza nocchiere, in gran tempesta,
> Non donna di provincie, ma bordello!

Cultural must precede political unity. For this, Dante's work laid the foundations, and his breadth of vision is without parallel in the history of medieval literature.

For Dante was by instinct an internationalist. He was impressed, as were many people in Western Europe, by the Roman empire, the Roman Catholic Church and the Latin language. He believed in the necessity and in the possibility of a world state, with pope and emperor working in harmony to produce and maintain an orderly Christendom; and before such great considerations any question of Italian nationality was of minor importance. But Italy as a whole was not interested in these matters. Italian literature of the eleventh and twelfth centuries, which is almost entirely in Latin, includes poems and annals which celebrate or relate the struggles of one city-state with another and show that the chief concern of Italians with the empire was to enlist its help on behalf of some particular commune. Vernacular poetry appeared in Italy at a comparatively late date, and her early medieval literature cannot be compared with that of France or England; Italy found outlet for her intellectual energy in the study of law and medicine for which her schools were famous throughout Europe and in the political and commercial intrigues conducted for the aggrandisement of individual city-states. Dante's enthusiasm for the empire and his hopes of a world state found very little response in his own country; these sentiments, indeed, led to his banishment. The Italians were interested in Rome, but in Rome republican, not imperial, constituted as were their own city-states. Similarly, the Italian humanists preferred the Latin of Italy to the Latin of the world: they praised Cicero, Virgil or Horace, not St Augustine or St Jerome; and recognising the descent of their mother tongue from that of the great classics, they assisted the movement for the standardisation of the Italian language. Thus this opposition to the universalist ideas of the middle ages became the starting-point of a sense of nationality connected with language.

The enthusiasm of Dante for the conception of a united Christendom under the joint direction of pope and emperor had become a dominant idea in Western Europe after the time of Charlemagne and was nowhere more potent than in the collection of states known as Germany. The belief throughout the Hohenstaufen period that Germany's duty and destiny was to sponsor this ideal and to work for internationalism, for the brotherhood and unity of the Christian peoples, may have inspired medieval Germany both intellectually and spiritually, but it was certainly the ruination of her political development. While other states were gradually consolidating their powers and resources and creating a sense of nationalism among their people, Germany was concerned with grandiose schemes which were deranged and thwarted by the ambitions of individual princes and by the struggles with the papacy. The want of national feeling is reflected in the general attitude to the German language long after medieval times; Germans were not ashamed to express their dislike for their mother tongue. Frederick II, perhaps the greatest of the Hohenstaufen emperors, preferred Italian, Arabic and Provençal to German; Charles V is said to have spoken German only to his dogs. This contempt persisted to the end of the eighteenth century; Frederick the Great never spoke German, if he could speak French; Wieland's complaint of German as the worst language in Europe was repeated by Schiller, who considered it too clumsy and rigid a tongue to be used for translating Virgil. Goethe declared:

> Nur ein einzig Talent bracht' ich der Meisterschaft nah,
> Deutsch zu schreiben, und so verderb' ich unglücklicher Dichter
> In dem schlechtesten Stoff leider nun Leben und Kunst.

A compromise speech or 'Dichtersprache' grew up among the exponents of the Minnesang in the late twelfth and early thirteenth centuries, a movement resembling that which produced troubadour poetical language in the South of France; but it was not until Luther translated the Bible that a standard German, practically the language of the Saxon chancery, was to replace the various dialects in use for literary purposes. Prejudice continued, as has been said, for long afterwards, and it was the work of the Romantic movement to arouse Germans to a pride in their language as a mark and possession of nationality.

Such a view of language is not, then, a characteristic of medieval thought. Before a language can be regarded as a national possession for which a people will fight and die, a nation has to be formed by geographical conditions and by political and social progress; a literature must grow and the means of standardising the language and circulating its literature must be provided; the invention of printing was indispensable to ensure circulation sufficiently wide and ready, to induce a people to believe that their literature was the expression of their society. Exceptions, no doubt, can be found. The Basques have long regarded their language with veneration; they consider that it was the tongue spoken in the Garden of Eden, and that all Basques will go to heaven, for the simple reason that the devil cannot tempt them, as he has never been able to learn Basque; anyone who has glanced at the Basque verb will be inclined to sympathise with the devil's difficulties. But the Basques have been a comparatively small community, sheltered in a mountainous region not greatly disturbed by the conquests and defeats which have shaken and rearranged Western Europe; nor have they ever shown any burning desire to extend the area of their occupation. A static society of this kind can maintain its language and character without dependence upon the stimulus of printed matter; similar considerations will explain, to some extent, the persistence of Welsh, Irish and Breton. German was in a very different position; while such a nation as France was concentrating and centralising its power, German effort was wasted and dissipated.

A certain similarity can be observed in the course of development which vernacular tongues in Western Europe have undergone. From a parent speech, whether Latin, Celtic, Germanic or any other, local dialects have been derived, differing from one another in varying degrees, but not so greatly as to make intercommunication impossible between the members of one group. One of these dialects then begins to extend its area, because the state in which it is spoken enjoys some advantage of geographical position, of political preponderance, or of denser population. This dialect may thus eventually become the standard speech of the country, as Francien or Castilian have respectively done, or a compromise between dialects may be secured, as in Germany. The invention of printing stabilised the predominant mode of speech, secured its position as the official and literary medium, and thereby reduced dialects which had once been its equal to the status of patois. The next step is to regard the official language as a national heritage and an expression of national character. This idea made slow progress, so long as the wars of religion continued; 'cujus regio, ejus religio' is the prevailing note of the sixteenth and seventeenth centuries; but the growth of literature and the spread of education consequent upon the greater multiplication of books increased its strength continually. The Romantic movement in the last years of the eighteenth and the beginning of the nineteenth centuries discovered the fact that the great vernaculars had a long history behind them, and that a wealth of literature providing material eminently attractive to romantic taste lay hidden in manuscripts known hitherto only by a few obscure scholars and antiquarians. Much of this literature was brought to light and an editorial technique was evolved; at the same time, attempts were made to analyse the history of linguistic development and to formulate its laws. The value of dialect and patois was appreciated by the philologist, interest in the linguistic past aroused respect for languages which seemed moribund, and efforts to revive them were made. For instance, Carles Aribau began the Catalan renaissance in 1833 with his *Oda a la Pàtria*; three years earlier Mistral was born. Many scholars and poets had worked to restore interest in Provençal before that date, but Mistral's poetic power and untiring energy carried that interest far beyond mere antiquarianism. Similar work was done in the German-speaking and Scandinavian countries. And then the discovery was made that language had a political significance.

Throughout the last hundred years that significance has been continually stressed. Germany has expelled most of the foreign terms, especially the French, which her language had hybridised. Eire has laid upon the schoolboy the burden of her ancient language (said to be unsuited to the needs of modern civilisation, but possessing an interesting antiquarian literature), because it was thought to be the symbol of a nationalist revival. Rhaeto-Romanisch, which had held out against the encroachments of German and Italian for antiquarian reasons, has now secured political recognition. Mistral's agitation for the teaching of Provençal in the schools of Southern France was rejected; concession might have produced a situation similar to that in Catalonia, where, as in the Basque provinces and Galicia, language has been the foundation upon which claims for autonomy and political decentralisation have been based. Latvia and Lithuania regarded their languages as one of the reasons for their political independence. A conqueror considers the existence of a native language as a source of danger; when Italy gained Southern Tirol, she proceeded to rename localities, to enforce the teaching of Italian in the schools, and to suppress German wherever possible. Thus we have reached a state of things inconceivable in the middle ages; wars are waged about language, prohibitions of language are issued, suppressions of language are practised. The medieval dictum, 'cujus regio, ejus religio' must be rewritten, 'cujus regio, ejus lingua'.

One of the greatest obstacles to the communication of ideas between different nationalities is diversity of language; to this, in the middle ages, was added difficulty of travel and intercourse. The latter barrier has been broken down; never, in the world's history, have the possibilities of inter-communication by land, sea and air been greater or more rapid and easy than modern invention has made them. Yet we are confronted by the paradoxical fact that the linguistic obstacles to communication are more formidable at the present time than at any previous period in the history of Western Europe. Economic nationalism has been used to strengthen them. Self-determination has been thought to imply self-sufficiency; political and economic independence were to go hand in hand. The confusion produced by the measures adopted to achieve this end, the tariff walls, the juggling with currencies, the maze of commercial pacts, agreements and treaties, produced at a time when technical progress had brought forth increased supplies in an abundance with which only some form of economic internationalism could deal, is a problem outside our scope. The fact remains that the linguistic argument has been constantly used to encourage the rage for political independence and self-sufficiency, at a time and in conditions when such independence can be secured only at the cost of terrific economic sacrifice.

CHAPTER IV

STYLE & CRITICISM

WHEN a vernacular has become sufficiently stabilised and wide-spread to produce literature, questions of style begin to arise: What is the best mode of expression? How can expression be modified to suit a particular subject or to appeal to a particular audience? What means can be discovered for attracting and holding attention or for securing applause? These were matters that had been discussed and analysed by rhetoricians long before medieval times, and many a medieval writer was brought up under their precepts. But before entering upon this subject, it is necessary to know in what sense the term 'style' is now generally used.

Obviously, the nature of the subject-matter and the character of the reader or audience must often dictate the character of the language used; to rewrite a proposition of Euclid in the manner of Gibbon or Carlyle would be to produce a result not only grotesque, but useless for its purpose; nor does a man of sense talk to his family as he would address a political meeting. If the appeal is made to intellect, the manner will not be that of an appeal to emotion.[1] Methodical Germany recognises a *Schriftsprache* and an *Umgangssprache*, which latter may be divided into a *Vortragssprache*, a *Verkehrssprache* and a *Familiensprache*, the respective manners of oratory, of official intercourse and of conversation. *Schrift-sprache*, the literary language, will include variations dependent upon subject-matter, and in every language which has reached the stage of nationality, these differences will be apparent in greater or less degree. The ancient rhetoricians were familiar with them and laid down rules for the teaching of them; these were elaborated in medieval times and were known as arts of style. Oratory and poetry had their appropriate styles, and careful analysis of the most famous poems and speeches had

[1] Habla un hombre en diferente estilo
del que tiene vulgar, quando aconseja,
persüade o aparta alguna cosa.
(Lope de Vega, *Arte Nuevo*, l. 255.)

evolved a body of rules and precepts, the observance of which was thought essential for success.

Thus we speak of a conversational or of an oratorical style with reference to the particular manner of delivery and choice of words which the occasion may demand. So medieval critics regarded style as a manner which could be changed at will, the change being determined by the nature of the subject with which the artist had to deal; even as a man invited to a party will change his working clothes for a more formal dress. But we also use the term to denote the expression of character in art or literature. A page of Carlyle can be easily recognised and distinguished from a page of Macaulay, though the subject-matter of both pages may be identical; twenty bars or less of music by Bach or Mendelssohn can be at once assigned to their respective composers by a competent musical critic, even at the first time of hearing the passages; unsigned pictures can be attributed to their artists, and this simply by the indications of style. The practised artist or writer stamps his own individuality upon his productions with unmistakable clarity, whether he means to do so or not; 'stylus virum arguit' said Sir Thomas Browne, and is followed by Buffon, 'le style est l'homme même'. Style in this sense is the revelation of personality; whether it is ugly or pleasing, depends upon the character of the writer. It cannot be analysed; it cannot be taught. Imitation of it may produce mannerisms or even parody; but the quality which marks the words of a great orator or the writing of a great author is wholly elusive; it has been regarded even as a gift from heaven. 'So true it is that the gods do not give every gracious gift to all, neither shapeliness, nor wisdom, nor skilled speech. For one man is feebler than another in presence, yet the god crowns his words with beauty, and men behold him and rejoice, and his speech runs surely on its way with a sweet modesty, and he shines forth among the gathering of the people and as he passes through the town men gaze on him as a god. Another again is like the deathless gods for beauty, but his words have no crown of grace about them; even as thou art in comeliness pre-eminent, nor could a god himself fashion thee better, but in wit thou art a weakling.'[1]

Those tricks in the art of speaking or writing which the medieval rhetoricians analysed and catalogued under the title of style should more properly be termed 'technique'. Buffon had realised the need for

1 Homer, *Od.* VIII, 170.

this distinction: 'le ton n'est que la convenance du style à la nature du sujet', but he did not develop the idea. It is a distinction which was unknown to the medievals; this is not to say that their writers failed to develop a personal style; no writer of any eminence can avoid revealing himself to those who know how to read. But the revelation was involuntary and unrecognised. Medieval criticism regarded creative work as a science; anyone who was willing to learn the complicated rules of the business could become a poet; the typical poet was a learned man who had the technique at his fingers' ends and not a rare and favoured person upon whom divine inspiration had descended. Such a man, indeed, was a hopeless case, unless he was willing to undergo the necessary training. Perspiration, the readiness to take pains, was more useful than inspiration. No one has put the matter more strongly than Dante: 'here let the folly of those stand confessed, who, innocent of art and knowledge and trusting to genius alone, rush forward to sing of the highest subjects in the highest style. Let them cease from such presumption, and if, in their natural sluggishness they are but geese, let them abstain from imitating the eagle soaring to the stars.' [1]

Boccaccio on this question follows his master: 'however deeply the poetic impulse stirs the mind to which it is granted, it very rarely accomplishes anything commendable, if the instruments by which its concepts are to be wrought out are wanting—I mean, for example, the precepts of grammar and rhetoric.' [2] Antonio de Tempo, who published his *Summa Artis Rithmici* in 1333, is of the same opinion: 'unum tamen loquor, quod non poterit aliquis esse bonus rithimator vulgaris, nisi saltem grammaticalibus studiis sit imbutus, et quanto melius alias liberales artes et alias scientias noverit positivas, tanto magis, si haec vulgaris dictaminis scientia eius ingenio placuerit, perfectus inter caeteros apparebit. Verumtamen quidam etiam qui non sunt aliqualiter literati ex industria sensus naturalis sciunt aliquos vulgares rithimos compilare, licet non habeant quam haberent, si saltem grammaticae notitiam aliquam habuissent.' [3]

1 *De Vulg. Eloq.* II, 4.

2 C. G. Osgood, *Boccaccio on Poetry*, Princeton University Press, 1930, p. 40.

3 *Collezione di opere inedite o rare*, XVIII, Bologna, 1869, p. 71. This opinion is repeated as late as 1572, by Jean de la Taille, *De l'art de la Tragédie* (*Les Ouvrages de l'Esprit*, ed. F. West, Manchester University Press, p. 30), who says that some poets 'font des choses si fades et malplaisantes qu'elles deussent faire rougir de honte les papiers mesmes, aux cerveaux desquels est entrée ceste sotte

The troubadour Peire Vidal (1170–1213?) is grateful for his early training:

> E s'eu sai.ren dir ni faire,
> ilh n'aia-l grat, que sciensa
> m'a donat e conoissensa,
> per qu'eu sia gaise chantaire.

(From *Ab l'alen tir vas me l'aire*) 'If I have any power to write or compose, let her (Provence) be thanked for it, who has given me learning and knowledge to make me a cheerful singer.'

Opinions are naturally discrepant and some troubadours laid stress upon the importance of inspiration, which Bernart de Ventadorn declared, in his case, to be due to love:

> Non es meravilha s'ieu chan
> mieilhs de nulh autre chantador,
> que plus mi tra.l cors vers amor
> e mieilhs sui faitz a son coman.

(Ed. Appel, p. 186; the song *Chantars no pot guaire valer* repeats the idea.) Giraut Riquier declared that inspiration is of divine origin:

> Car dicus los vol onrar
> el mon de tal saber
> c'om no.l poiri' aver
> per ren d'ome carnal.
> E en totz sabers val
> autres bona doctrina,
> mas si dieus non aizina
> home en comensar
> al saber de trobar,
> ja nulh temps no l'aura.

'God wills to honour poets in the world with knowledge that a man could not get from any other mortal man. In all other branches of learning, good teaching is precious, but if God does not endow a man at the outset with knowledge of poetry, he will never gain it' (Mahn, *Werke*, III, p. 180; dated 1275).

opinion de penser qu'on naisse et qu'on devienne naturellement excellent en cest art, avec une fureur divine, sans suer, sans feuilleter, sans choisir l'invention, sans limer les vers, et sans noter en fin de compte qu'il y a beaucoup de rymeurs et peu de poëtes'.

The word 'style' has extended its connotation in our times; it is used by the modern world to describe the exploits of the cricketer, the oarsman, and even the burglar. But in these cases we may mean, either that the athlete in question has a complete mastery of the technique of the game, or that he is a genius whose power transcends this technique and makes his performance peculiarly his own, or both of these points may be simultaneously in our mind. But in discussing medieval criticism, and medieval opinions upon style, we are concerned only with matters of technique, as were the compilers of treatises upon the subject.[1] For instance: 'here begins the fifth part of our work, in which we are to expound and explain certain precepts and instructions to teach those anxious to compose in *Romans* in what manner they will be able to *trobar e dictar*, notwithstanding that their nature may be too insensitive to accomplish this (*non contrastan, que lor natura sia trop dura ad aysso far*)'. 'We now proceed to show how we can find a subject for a poem, when we have no subject ready to hand. In this mode of composition, we must proceed as do the weavers, who first prepare and warp their threads, and then weave the cloth.'[2] William Morris described his writing of poetry in almost the same terms.[3]

It was a definition in full consonance with the ideals of the middle ages which valued craftsmanship above all things. Poetry was composed to be heard, not to be read; it was intended to give pleasure to the ear, and as the regular recurrence of rhythm has been found to be the simplest means of attaining this end, medieval poetry may be

---

1 Cp. Sir William Craigie, *The Art of Poetry in Iceland*, Taylorian Lecture, 1937, p. 3: 'throughout the centuries the poets of Iceland have regarded poetry as being above all things an *art*, an exercise in, or an exhibition of, skill in the handling of words and metres. In other words, they have considered that the ability to make poetry was not so much a natural gift as an accomplishment, the result of knowledge and practice, in which success could only be attained by the strict observance of established rules of composition.' The Arcipreste de Hita regarded emotion as a positive hindrance to poetical composition:

'Dize un filósofo, en su libro se nota,
Que pesar e tristeza el engeño enbota.'

(*Libro de Buen Amor*, l. 1518; cp. ll. 1507 and 1575.)

2 M. Gatien-Arnoult, *Las Leys d'Amors*, Toulouse, 1843, III, pp. 360 and 377.

3 'That talk of inspiration is sheer nonsense; there is no such thing. It is a mere matter of craftsmanship.' And again, 'if a chap can't compose an epic poem while he's weaving tapestry, he'd better shut up; he'll never do any good at all'.

defined, in its formal aspect, as language in recurrent rhythmical form. By the use of rhythm we mean the introduction into language of a principle of proportion in the arrangement of words. In conversation or writing upon technical subjects we do not expect to find this principle fully operative; the order of words is there dictated by the sequence of the argument, and any interference with that order will distract the listener's attention. But when a man speaks upon any highly passionate theme, his voice rises and falls, while his words arrange themselves in obedience to an irresistible sense of order; the expression of his passion thus falls under control and regulation; spasmodic or confused utterance, with its unfavourable effects upon the listener, is avoided. In such a case, as in the peroration of a political orator, the rhythm of the language is irregular; when, however, the recurrence of a voice modulation can be anticipated with some certainty by the hearer, rhythm becomes metre, and such rhythmical language becomes in form, either verse or poetry, which recurrence may be reinforced by the use of rime. It is from the regularity of the recurrence that much of the attraction of poetry is derived; hence it is important that this regularity should be easily perceptible to the listener, and that he should be able to anticipate it in thought.

Medieval poetry must thus be capable of recitation; if it could not stand this test, the poet was regarded as a bungler. These conditions have been altered by the printed page; the reader need not keep a rime sequence or a rhythmical system in his head; if these are not immediately clear, he can read the opening stanza a second time. The poet can use rimes for the eye (sword-word) as well as for the ear,[1] a license forbidden to the medieval; no self-respecting troubadour would rime a close with an open vowel. The modern printer places each line successively in the middle of the page and indents lines to show the rime correspondence; the medieval scribe was always ready, as parchment was expensive, to write lyric poetry as though it were prose, though he would put a stop between each line, if he were a conscientious copyist. His punctuation consisted of a full stop and an inverted semicolon, used for little more than to show where a sentence came to an end; modern punctuation is used not only to show the syntactical construction of a sentence but to indicate rhetorical values. Compare, for instance,

(a) The prisoner then murdered his grandmother with a meat-axe.

1 See Appendix C.

(*b*) The prisoner then murdered his grandmother, *with a meat-axe*!
(*a*) is a reporter's newspaper statement; (*b*) is the delivery of it by a prosecuting counsel.

Or again,
   These 'gentlemen' (?) seem to have forgotten the rules of polite society.
         Entombed within this grave a lawyer lies,
         Who, Fame assureth us, was just and wise!

The final exclamation mark suggests that the credibility of 'Fame' is open to suspicion. These typographical devices, whether they be legitimate or not, were far beyond the scope of the medieval scribe, and entirely outside of his experience were the visual associations which we bring to the reading of poetry; the 'lay-out' of the page is the salvation of the latest 'modern' poetry.

   By the curb towards the edge of the flagging,
   A knife-grinder works at his wheel sharpening a great knife,
   Bending over he carefully holds it to the stone, by foot and knee,
   With measured tread he turns rapidly, as he presses with light but firm hand,
   Forth issue then in copious golden jets
   Sparkles from the wheel.   (Walt Whitman.)

So far as form is concerned, there seems to be no reason why this extract should not be printed as 'prose-poetry', or 'poetic prose'. Poetry of this kind can be produced from any source of rhythmical prose; the following is taken at random from the writings of Walter Pater:

            One seems diminished to nothing at all,
            Amid the grand waves,
            Wave upon wave, of patiently wrought stone;
            The daring height, the daring severity
            Of the innumerable long, upward, ruled lines,
            Rigidly bent
            Just at last, in due place,
            Into the reserved grace of the perfect
            Gothic Arch.

Pater wrote and printed this passage as prose; an age subjected to the visual illusions of print may well regard it as poetry no worse than much that comes forth under this title. We are not here concerned with reasons that may exist for the denunciation of the trammels of rime and rhythm; the point is, that this technique, which seems to be of little interest to some moderns, was of primary importance to medieval poets.

Such a difference between medieval and modern standards of taste was inevitable before the invention of printing. To savour the finer points of literary style, as we understand it, to appreciate the exact choice of words, the cadence of phrases and even the logical sequence of ideas, we require to read and re-read the matter presented to us. But it was not to a reading public that the medieval writer appealed. An unlettered audience cannot be treated tenderly; points must be vigorously emphasised; statements must be repeated, variety of diction must be introduced. The story-teller will present his characters in person, in conversation with each other, and by change of voice, intonation and gesture will make them live in the minds of his hearers; he must be something of an actor as well as a narrator. The modern concert audience does not expect to hear all the words of a song, and even if the hearer grasps them, a feeble lyric is redeemed, in his opinion, by a good tune and a trained voice. But tune and words were of equal importance in medieval times, and the troubadour who produced 'bos sos e paubres motz' was regarded as a second-rate performer. No one could leave a recitation of any kind with the comfortable consciousness that he could read it all in print in the next day's newspaper or the next month's magazine; if its intention were not grasped upon the spot, it was gone for ever, so far as he was concerned. Hence the distinction of styles, in the medieval sense of the term, and the analysis of figures of speech and ornaments of rhetoric was important to an extent which cannot now be readily realised, for the technique of the speaker or reciter of his own works is not and cannot be that of the writer who proposes to approach his public in cold print and to derive royalties from their appreciation. The quality that we now call style was, in medieval times, largely provided by the personality of the speaker or reciter, and the appeal of style was to the ear alone.

Giraldus Cambrensis, for instance, refers to the eulogies passed upon his 'style' (Rolls Series, vol. i, p. 80) 'Coepit librum (Topographia Hibernica) valde commendare et stylum ipsius tractandique modum multis laudibus extollere.... Ad haec injunxit ei archiepiscopus ut gratiam styli egregii sibi a Deo collati vacuam esse non permitteret.' 'Style' here meant a mastery of the rhetorical rules and ornaments. The admiration of Giraldus for his friend Walter Map, whose wit he described as 'sales saporifero sapientiae sale conditos', is enough to show the character of his literary ideals, for every precept of the rhetoricians can be abundantly illustrated from the *De Nugis Curialium* of Map, no less than from the writings of Giraldus himself. Gervase of Canterbury began his chronicle by emphasising the difference between chronicle and history in point of style. 'Historicus diffuse et eleganter incedit, cronicus vero simpliciter graditur et breviter. Projicit historicus ampullas et sesquipedalia verba; cronicus vero, silvestrem musam tenui meditatur avena'. The historian may 'audientes vel legentes dulci sermone et eleganti demulcere'; the chronicler's business is to recount a succession of events under accurate dates. Some chroniclers disregard this difference. 'Sunt autem plurimi qui, cronicas vel annales scribentes, limites suos excedunt.... Dum enim cronicam compilare cupiunt, historici more incedunt, et quod breviter sermoneque humili de modo scribendi dicere debuerant, verbis ampullosis aggravare conantur.' This adaptation of style to subject matter also held good for correspondence. Thus Grosseteste, in 1245, apologised to Henry III for the style of a previous letter: 'licet forte per imperitiam nostram non ita rhetorice scripserimus ut pro qualitate materiae eloquentia rhetorica requireret'.[1]

Hence, some attention must be given to the rules of style as formulated by the rhetoricians.

The chief early medieval writers who produced treatises upon the art of composition were Matthieu de Vendôme, whose *Ars Versificatoria* was written before 1175, Geoffroi de Vinsauf, whose *Poetria Nova* is dated about 1210, Gervais de Melkley, *Ars Versificaria*, Everard the German, the date of whose *Laborintus* is uncertain, but was before 1280, and John of Garland, an Englishman, who studied at Oxford and Paris, was a professor at Toulouse from 1229 to 1231, after which he returned to Paris and apparently spent the rest of his life in that city or neighbourhood; he was the author of some dozen treatises, and more have been wrongly attributed to him; the date of his *Poetria* is not known.

1 Gervase of Canterbury, Rolls Series, vol. I, p. 87. On this point, see below, p. 62. Grosseteste, Rolls Series, *Epistolae*, p. 352.

The doctrines formulated by these and other writers are based in part upon the *De Inventione* of Cicero, the *Ars Poetica* of Horace and the *Rhetorica ad Herennium* of Cornificius; the close study and analysis of texts as expounded at the universities of Orléans and Paris provided material for illustrating and expanding the classical principles. By the middle of the thirteenth century teachers were in general agreement upon the main body of rhetorical instruction.[1]

The first subject for consideration is the arrangement of material. In the case of a narrative, two methods are recognised, to follow either the 'natural' order of events, or to choose an 'artificial' order; for the latter case, the type is Virgil, who begins his *Aeneid* with the shipwreck of his hero on the African coast and then makes him relate the previous course of events in the next two books of the epic. The 'natural' order is that recommended in various *artes dictaminis*, treatises on letter writing, and is applicable to subjects other than narrative; here the arrangement will be, the exordium, the statement of the case or narrative, confirmation or refutation of any points for discussion and conclusion. Some authorities recommend the author to begin with a proverb or generalisation; thus Benoît de Sainte-Maure begins the *Roman de Troie* with a reference to Solomon. Garnier de Pont-Sainte-Maxence begins his life of St Thomas of Canterbury:

> Tuit li fysiciën ne sunt ades bon mire;
> Tuit clerc ne sevent pas bien chanter ne bien lire;
> Asquanz des trovëurs faillent tost a bien dire.

and proceeds to justify his own undertaking. Other means of attracting attention are appeals to curiosity:

> Seygnours, escotez un petit
> Si orrez un tres bon desduit.
> (F. Michel, *La Riote du Monde*; *le Roi d'Angleterre et le Jongleur d'Ely*.)

> Qui bien commence et qui bien sert
> Guerredon au doble desert.
> (Gui de Cambrai, *Barlaam et Josaphat*.)

---

1 The best account of literary technique in the middle ages is E. Faral, *Les Arts Poétiques du XIIe et du XIIIe Siècle*, Paris, 1924. G. Mari, *I Trattati Medievali di Ritmica Latina*, Milano, 1899, partly covers the same ground.

suggests that both audience and reciter will get their reward. The exordium may be in the nature of a prologue, summarising the matter of the narrative, as in *Girart de Roussillon*; presumably, those who did not wish to listen could withdraw at the end of the prologue and leave others undisturbed. As for the body of the narrative, the precepts of the rhetoricians were naturally not observed with any exactitude; many narrative poems seem to us wanting in a due sense of proportion, and the unity of action is not always apparent. But they were not intended for a reading public; they were to be recited in episodes, so long as the hearers would listen, and the medieval equivalent of 'to be continued in our next' would naturally occur at a moment of high interest or excitement.

As an instance *Erec et Enide* by Chrétien de Troyes may be taken. Chrétien was a supreme artist in this particular *genre*, the *roman d'aventure*, which reached its high-water mark in the latter half of the twelfth century. The story is composed of three episodes which can be subdivided. It begins with the account of an insult offered to Arthur's queen, which Erec goes forth to avenge; he meets Enide, defeats the insolent lord and sends him back to make submission to Arthur. Then follows the account of his return with Enide, their reception and marriage. This matter occupies 2292 lines of octosyllabic verse, which are divisible as 1243 and 1049 lines respectively. The second episode relates Erec's 'recreance', from which state of slothful uxoriousness he is stirred to go forth upon new adventures; these are told in lines 2293 to 4938, and can again be divided into two sub-episodes, the departure, subsequent encounters, collapse under excessive numbers and transport to a castle for recovery, in (lines 2293–3662) 1369 lines; secondly, the behaviour of the castle owner to Enide, the hero's recovery and return (3662–4938), 1276 lines. The third episode runs from 4939–6958, 2019 lines, and relates the adventure of 'Joie de la Cour', which is not obviously divisible, though a halt, which would leave the audience breathless for more, might be made at line 5739, dividing this episode into 801 and 1218 lines respectively. How much recitation at a time was either demanded by the audience or supported by the reciter is a matter of sheer conjecture;[1] but the 'lay-out' of the matter indicates that convenient halting-places were

1 Speculation upon the subject can be found in Gautier, *Les Epopées françaises*, III, p. 232.

clearly marked, as in a *feuilleton* which doles out a story for daily consumption.

The character of the audience is indicated by the style and matter of the narrative; Chrétien composed for a feudal aristocracy. 'Dans la salle du château, pour la veillée, autour de la cheminée héraldique, où le tronc d'arbre se calcine sur les chenets, autour du jongleur à la vielle, à la harpe, ou à la rote, ou autour de celui ou celle qui sait lire, se rassemblent des chevaliers ayant laissé haubert et heaume pour revêtir le pelisson fourré et qui, sur des peaux, s'étendent auprès des dames en bliauts de soie, aux longues tresses pendantes.'[1] A work intended for performance under such conditions must not be judged by modern standards. A critical reader will be struck by inconsequences or irrelevancies; the tournament, for instance, with which the marriage festivities conclude, adds nothing to the story nor to the characters of the actors; it is there because the audience liked tournaments; they were interested in technical accounts of professional ability, which could stir the ambition of the young; the same may be said of descriptions of warriors' equipment and ladies' dresses. There is a certain monotony in the various combats which Erec wages, while the third episode might be omitted altogether without damaging the story, though Chrétien could defend it on the ground that it reinforced the central theme, the conquest of 'recreance', the existence of which secures a certain unity of action. Such defects were not apparent to those who heard the story episodically, and whose chief requirement was a momentary excitement derived from following the adventures of characters with whom they were in sympathy. If the story was set in a dim Celtic past, the life of which they heard was, from a social point of view, their own or one to which they aspired, with its castles, feasts, rich suits of armour and bejewelled dresses, bedecking men and women of noblest birth, whose courtesy was as elaborate as their courage was indomitable.

When the subject-matter had been provided and the general arrangement of it had been settled, medieval rhetoricians enjoined various devices for its elaboration and development. Eight of these were generally recognised. The first was known as 'interpretatio' and 'expolitio', and consisted in saying the same thing in different terms, or varying expression by a change of voice, or of sentence construction,

1 G. Cohen, *Chrétien de Troyes et son Œuvre*, Paris, 1931, p. 109.

i.e. using an interrogative sentence, or advancing a negative which is immediately to be refuted; e.g. *Erec*, ll. 1220 ff.:

> 'Mout vos donai buen consoil hier,
> Quant jel vos loai a atandre.
> Por ce fet il buen consoil prandre.'
> Li rois respont: 'N'est mie fable,
> Ceste parole est veritable:
> Qui croit consoil, n'est mie fos.'

or *Jaufre*, ll. 3059 ff.:

> E.l vergiers es d'una pulcella
> que a nom Brunissens la bella,
> e sos castels a nom Monbrun.
> E no.us cuidetz ges que sol un
> n'aia, q'enantz n'a d'autres motz,
> mas Monbruns es lo caps de totz
> e deu aver la seignoria.
> Mas la pulcella non avia
> paire ni maire ni marit
> ni fraire, car tuit son fenit
> e mort e d'est segle passat;
> e ela ten la eretat,
> que no i a nulh autre seinor.[1]

'And the garden belongs to a damsel whose name is Brunissen the fair and her castle is called Monbrun. And do not think that she has but one castle; on the contrary she has many others, but Monbrun is the chief of all and has the lordship. But the damsel had neither father, mother nor husband nor brother, for all are ended and dead and gone from this world, and she holds the inheritance, for there is no other lord.'

These tricks naturally degenerate to mere padding and the use of *chevilles* and set phrases; but the fact is supported by wide experience that to get an idea into the heads of the average audience, it must be repeated three times at least and the rhetoricians provided recipes for performing the operation artistically.[2] Another form of 'amplification'

1 Appel, *Provenzalische Chrestomathie*, p. 14.
2 Cp. Léon Gautier on the question of repetitions in the *chansons de geste* (*Les Epopées françaises*, 1, pp. 221 ff.).

was that known as 'frequentatio', a catalogue of descriptive phrases, more or less metaphorical; e.g. *Erec*, ll. 541 ff.:

> Quant je ai delez moi ma fille,
> Tot le mont ne pris une bille.
> C'est mes deduiz, c'est mes deporz.
> C'est mes solaz, c'est mes conforz.
> C'est mes avoirs, c'est mes tresors.

Twenty lines of asseveration in this style conclude the Provençal *Jaufre* (ll. 8334 ff.) and similar examples constantly occur.

The second and third means of 'amplification' were periphrasis and comparison or the use of simile; the former is too common to need illustration. The latter appears but sparsely in the *chansons de geste*, and then in simple form; the old man's beard is 'white as hawthorn in flower'. The elaborate simile of Homer or Virgil appears to have lost favour at an early date and was little used after the eleventh century.

Apostrophe, the fourth device, is of early occurrence; e.g. *Alexis*, l. 141, when his mother apostrophises the deserted room:

> Chambre, dist ele, ja mais n'estras parede
> ne ja ledece n'iert en tei demenede!

Addresses to Death, Love, Fortune, etc., and to inanimate objects are common enough, and combine this means of 'amplification' with the fifth, personification, which was worked almost to death in medieval literature.

Of greater importance was the 'digression'. This might be a temporary abandonment of the narrative for the purpose of moralising, explaining technicalities, or describing scenes and objects of interest; the last-mentioned form of digression is regarded as a device worthy of separate treatment. The second use of digression was to keep in hand the threads of the plot; a subordinate action might anticipate in time the proceedings of the main actors, and clarity be thus secured. The resumption of the main thread must be clearly marked; e.g. *Erec*, l. 1244:

> Or redevons d'Erec parler,
> Qui ancor an la place estoit,
> Ou la bataille feite avoit.

Under this heading may come the use of direct speech and of dialogue, which was common in the *chansons de geste*, and was used with especial dexterity by Chrétien de Troyes. This device[1] allowed the poet to represent a character as discussing with himself a situation or his own feelings, to give the opinions of a crowd in their own words upon the course of a tournament or the bearing of a champion, to reveal and illustrate character in dialogue with another. It provided opportunities for the reciter or reader to speak in character, somewhat after the fashion of the modern 'diseuse', and to vary the monotony of the long assonanced 'laisse' in the *chanson de geste* or of the rhymed octosyllabic couplet in the *roman d'aventure*.[2]

These are matters concerned with the arrangement and adornment of subject-matter and are preliminary to the main question, that of style. The Ciceronian doctrine distinguished three styles, *gravis, mediocris* and *attenuatus*, the difference between which depended upon the orator and his capacity; when we reach the medieval rhetoricians, this meaning has been considerably extended and style is determined by the nature of the subject-matter; John of Garland states, 'item sunt tres styli secundum tres status hominum: pastorali vitae convenit stylus humilis, agricolis mediocris, gravis gravibus personis quae praesunt pastoribus et agricolis', in obvious reference to the *Bucolics, Georgics* and *Aeneid* of Virgil, which were set out as models of the three styles in the 'Virgilian Wheel'.[3] The difference between styles in the twelfth century was marked by the constructions and even more by the vocabulary used, which must be suited to the subject-matter. The rhetoricians of that time classified 'mots sénateurs et mots roturiers', as strictly as did French critics of the seventeenth century. A further division of the subject is made in the 'ornaments of style', which can be of two kinds, 'difficult' and 'easy'. The difficult kind of ornament consists in the use of words in senses other than their common meaning, and this by means of

1 Alfons Hilka, *Die Direkte Rede als stilistisches Kunstmittel in den Romanen des Kristian von Troyes*, Halle, 1903, analyses this subject very thoroughly.

2 Examples from the *roman courtois* are more cogent than those from earlier poems, as a more refined public might be expected to have a greater facility in the art of reading. M. Wilmotte (*L'Epopée française*, Paris, 1939, chap. IV) has shown the extent to which the early epics, *Alexis*, and the first examples of literature display an acquaintance with the precepts of the rhetoricians which suggests an education in their schools or a knowledge of 'classical' methods, based upon a study of Virgil and other classical texts.

3 Faral, p. 87. For similar allegorical interpretations of the books of Virgil, see Comparetti, *Virgil in the Middle Ages*.

'tropes' which include such figures of speech as metaphor, antithesis, periphrasis, synecdoche, and allegory, rhetorical devices of which examples are common and easily found. The easy kind of ornament is chiefly concerned with the so-called colours of rhetoric; these are figures of speech and it is not always obvious why a distinction should be made between some of them and the 'difficult' ornaments. The figures enumerated in the medieval treatises are some thirty or forty in number and include such obvious and much used devices as the repetition of a word for emphasis, the use of exclamation, of synonyms, description by contraries and contrasts or by reduplication of points described. The device known as *annominatio*, which depended upon similarity between words, was a favourite, and often descended to the word play now known as punning. *Mare*, *amare* and *amarus* provided easy material for this conceit.

> E pos guida.l ferm' estela lusens
> las naus que van perilhan per la mar,
> ben degra mi cilh qui.l sembla, guidar;
> qu'en la mar sui per leis profondamens
> tan esvaratz etc.

'And since the steadfast bright star guides the ships which go their dangerous ways through the sea, she who is like the star should guide me, for on her account I am so deeply whelmed in the sea (which the hearers can interpret as *en l'amar*) that I shall perish without help.'[1]

Chrétien de Troyes carries the word play through some twenty lines of *Cligés* (ll. 545 ff.):

> Mes ne set, por quoi il le font
> Fors que por la mer, ou il sont.
> Espoir bien s'an aparceüst,
> Se la mers ne la deceüst;
> Mes la mers l'angingne et deçoit
> Si qu'an la mer l'amer ne voit;
> Qu'an la mer sont, et d'amer vient,
> Et s'est amers il maus, quis tient.

'(The queen sees them sigh and shudder) but does not know why they do it, unless it be on account of the sea on which they are sailing. Perhaps she would

1 de Lollis, *Sordello*, no. 20, l. 20; his note gives other examples. Gotfrid von Strassburg copied it in *Tristràn*, ll. 11,990–12,000.

have perceived it, if the sea had not misled her; but it is the sea which baffles and deceives her, so that amid the seasickness she sees not the heart sickness. For they are at sea and heart sickness is the cause of their plight and heart bitterness of the ill that grips them.'

As has been said, devices of this kind are less common in the *chansons de geste*. These were composed for audiences who were chiefly interested in movement and action, battles, conquests and defeats, and the historic figures concerned in them. Hence there is a certain sameness in twelfth-century epics and the modern reader is naturally annoyed by the repeated use of formulae and set phrases. 'Ces clichés sont nombreux, fréquents et d'une banalité désespérante dès le début du xiime siècle; ils rendent la lecture de nos vieux poèmes souvent fastidieuse. Ce serait toutefois se méprendre que d'en faire un grief trop dur aux auteurs, dont ils secondent la mémoire, tandis qu'ils ne déplaisaient pas plus aux auditeurs que la synonymie exagérée dans l'emploi du vocabulaire ne dut choquer les lecteurs les plus délicats des romanciers d'alors, même les plus estimés, d'un Chrétien de Troyes par exemple. Sur tous ces points, comme aussi sur la valeur musicale des récitations du temps, il nous est totalement impossible d'arriver à une estimation juste de la portée esthétique des œuvres littéraires.'[1] This is very well said, but even greater emphasis might have been laid upon the fact that these works were not composed to be read and must not be judged from a reader's literary point of view. Repetition of formulae and 'clichés' is a feature of most primitive epics, from Homer onwards. The audience expected it, as children expect it in fairy tales; 'antiquitas saeculi, juventus mundi'.

Repetition, in different forms, has been a characteristic of epic poetry from Homer onwards. The repeated use of set formulae for the common actions of life, eating, sleeping, fighting, etc., was accepted as a convention; but poets who composed for public recitation were also aware of the rhetorical value of repetition as a means of increasing dramatic effect and of driving home their points. In the early epic, composed in assonant *laisses* of varying length, the device was used in several ways; there were the *laisses similaires*, in which an action was described twice or three times over in different terms in following *laisses*; two *laisses* might also be linked together by giving in the first lines of one a summary of the transaction described in the preceding *laisse*. Attempts have

[1] Wilmotte, p. 169, n. 2. A list of *chevilles* is given by P. Meyer, *Raoul de Cambrai*, A.T.F., Paris, 1882, p. lviii.

been made to discover some system of procedure;[1] but every poet who used the trick had his own methods; the author of the *Chanson de Roland* made more systematic use of this repetitive method than did other poets, whose practice of it in the majority of cases appears to have been haphazard. If, as has been supposed, the *laisse* was originally a lyric form adapted to the purposes of epic poetry, the chief difficulty in its use was to preserve a connection between one *laisse* and the next, a difficulty not diminished by the fact that the poem was sung, probably to some instrumental accompaniment, and that a change of melody may have taken place with each change of assonance, to avoid monotony. The word *AOI* in the *Chanson de Roland* and the short line of six syllables in the epics of the William of Orange cycle, as also the four-syllable lines which end the verse sections of *Aucassin et Nicolette*, have been interpreted as indications that the end of the *laisse* had been reached. If the melody was then changed, or if a short interlude was performed, the connection of the narrative might be lost or confused by the audience. Hence the practice of repeating an important incident in different words, or of summarising in the first lines of a new *laisse* the event narrated in the preceding *laisse*, or of repeating the last line of one *laisse* as the first line of the next. The first method may extend over two or even three *laisses* (e.g. *Roland*, nos. XL, XLI, XLII). More common is the summary, which is intended to pick up the thread of the narrative. In *Girart de Roussillon* (l. 7919), Girart and his wife took refuge with 'un lucrer felun' and his 'felonesse muller', who turned him out of his room when he was ill and forced him, like Alexis, to sleep under the stairs:

> Il lo fest devalar de son palaz
> en l'arvol d'un celer desoz uns graz.
> Aiqui a la contesse dolent solaz.

The following *laisse* begins:

> Girarz iaz en l'arvol, n'i a servent
> fors sa muller qui.l sert molt bonement.

Repetition was also used to emphasise particular points of interest. The monk whom Girart sent to open communications with Charles

1 The subject has been examined by M. K. Pope, *Modern Language Review*, VII, p. 352; IX, p. 41; X, p. 310. Also by W. Mulertt, *Laissenverbindung und Laissenwiederholung in der. Chansons de Geste*, Romanistische Arbeiten, VII, Halle, 1918.

(l. 6841) was harshly received and threatened with mutilation; the *laisse* ends:

> E.l moinges, quant l'oit, vougre esser loin.

The next *laisse* repeats the scene and ends:

> Li monges, quant l'oit, vougre estre estorz.

Later:

> E.l monges, quant l'auit, ne dis que non,
> Mas loinaz se vougre estre denant Carlon.

These repetitions work up to the climax of his panic departure, when he is allowed to go:

> Devalet per l'eschale plus que lo pas.

So in *Boeve de Haumtone*, when the giant Escopart appears, *laisse* CXXXII begins:

> Le veylen estoit mult grant e mult fers.

The next *laisse*:

> E le vilen estoit grant e metailez.

and the next:

> 'Di moi, velein', dist Boves le vailant,
>   pur icel deu en quey estes creant,
>   ou fustes vus ne e de quele gent?'

Escopart has a useful part to play and the poet is anxious that the hearers should have a clear idea of him.

  These repetitions may also have been an aid to the memory of the performer, by helping to fix in his mind the succession of incidents. The device finds its full development in the *laisses similaires*; Miss Pope sees it as a continuation of ballad methods with their refrains and repetitions of half stanzas; others have hinted at ecclesiastical influence, in imitation of antiphonal chanting or the parallelism of Hebrew psalmody. In any case, recipes for working it are given by the rhetoricians under the title of Amplification, which proceeds by 'interpretatio' and 'expolitio'; thus Geoffroi de Vinsauf:[1]

>   Si facis amplum,
> Hoc primo procede gradu: sententia cum sit
> Unica, non uno veniat contenta paratu,
> Sed variet vestes et mutatoria sumat;
> Sub verbis aliis praesumpta resume; repone
> Pluribus in clausis unum; multiplice forma
> Dissimuletur idem; varius sis et tamen idem.

1 Faral, p. 204.

Rhetorical matter in our own day, however successful it may have been as oratory, often makes dull reading; on the other hand, speeches that read well can be wearisome when delivered. There is plenty of political wisdom in sound literary form in the speeches of Burke, but in the House of Commons, Burke is said to have been a dinner bell. The country parson who lived far from banks and kept his reserve of banknotes in a volume of Tillotson's sermons, explained this habit on the ground that if a burglar broke into the vicarage, it was unlikely that he would want to read sermons, but that if he did, the last preacher he would choose would be Tillotson; yet Tillotson had much repute as a pulpit orator in his day. Rhetoric depends as much upon the speaker as upon the matter, and at no period of literary history can it be judged solely as literature. We know and can know very little of medieval methods of delivery; but it is at least certain that the methods in vogue would not have persisted, had they not been to the taste of audiences.

The case of lyric poetry is different from that of epic. Here the influence of Southern France was paramount; lyrical forms had here been elaborated at an earlier date than elsewhere in Western Europe and their influence upon other literatures was profound. The characteristics of lyric poetry are usually thought to be simplicity and spontaneity; a lyric is concerned with the expression of one thought or idea which comes unbidden from the heart and is clothed in words of simple and unrestrained emotion. The Provençal lyric schools can provide examples of lyrics in this style; but convention soon became paramount and technique took the place of emotion. From the earliest times, two poetical schools are found in opposition, the *trobar clus*, the obscure or close, subtle style of composition (also known as *car, ric, oscur, sotil, cobert*) and the *trobar clar* (*leu, leugier, plan*), the clear, light, easy, straightforward style.[1] The method of *trobar clus* is stated by Raimbaut d'Aurenga thus:

> Cars, bruns et teinz motz entrebesc
> Pensius pensanz. . . .

'I intertwine, thoughtfully thoughtful, words that are rare, dàrk and coloured.'

---

1 On this subject most of the relevant literature is noted by Jeanroy, *La Poésie lyrique des Troubadours*, Paris, 1934, II, pp. 32 ff. See also P. Andraud, *Quae judicia de litteris fecerint Provinciales*, Paris, 1902.

Strange turns of expression, unusual words, sometimes coined for the occasion, difficult rimes and stanza schemes of great complexity were the means by which the exponent of the *trobar clus* attempted, and often successfully, to hide his meaning from the vulgar herd. This was one method of revivifying the well-worn tale of love, a subject obligatory upon the troubadour and by no means inexhaustible. A further reason for obscurity may be due to the fact that the *chanso* was a love song addressed to a married lady; and though in many cases it contained compliments purely conventional, however exaggerated to modern ideas, the fact remains that the sentiments expressed might as easily be those of veritable passion, and, in view of a husband's existence, obscurity had a utility of its own. Peire d'Auvergne gives as a reason for obscurity of style, 'he is pleasing to me who proceeds to sing with words shut up and obscure, to which a man is afraid to do violence'; the 'violence' apprehended is that of the *joglar* who might spoil a composition by incompetence of delivery, or by interpolating allusions or alterations of his own. A complicated stanza was a safeguard against such mishandling; the case of Dante's *terza rima* will occur to every student.

There is, however, much probability that such a style was not of troubadour invention. The medieval rhetoricians, as has been said, had distinguished three styles and had analysed their characteristics, the *gravis*, *mediocris* and *humilis*. The weighty, lofty, noble and courtly style was marked by complication of construction, ornament of 'difficult' character, and a choice of suitable vocabulary. Such ideals may easily lead to exaggerations and obscurity; a tradition arose that an elevated and difficult style was aristocratic.[1] At all times the uneducated or half-educated classes of society have been prone to believe that the use of sonorous phrases, unusual words and involved sentence construction is indicative of a high degree of mental power. Carolingian times were not free from this obsession. Hincmar, archbishop of Rheims[2], wrote to a namesake or relative, vigorously criticising this degradation of style.

1 It has been suggested that the origin of the obscure style is to be found in the so-called 'Asianismus', the turgid and decorative style of the late Greek sophists and rhetoricians, continued in early medieval Latin and known as the 'gallicanus cothurnus', which attracted the attention of early writers in vernacular tongues. But the fact that a chronological succession of stylistic movements can be observed is not evidence of a causal connection between them.

2 Quoted by A. Viscardi, *Studi Medievali*, VII (1934), pp. 151 ff.

'Verba quoque obstrusa et undecunque per glossulas collecta et sine ratione posita quae in hoc scripto tuo posuisti, sicut et in aliis domino regi et mihi olim directis congessisti redarguunt te tipo iactantiae cum dicat Apostolus: vocum novitates devita. Et: malo quinque verba loqui in ecclesia ad aedificationem, quam decem milia verborum in lingua. Qui enim lingua in qua natus es non solum non loqui, verum nec intelligere nisi per interpretem potes, cum subpeterent sufficienter verba latina quae in his locis ponere poteras ubi graeca et obstrusa et interdum scotica et alia barbara ut tibi visum fuit notata atque corrupta posuisti.... Hunc namque morem etiam a pueritia habuisti in his quae te dictare rogabam, maxime autem in versibus et in figuris porphiriacis in quibus verba linguae alienae atque obstrusa impropria et utilitate sensus carentia, quae nec ipse intellegebas, studiose ponebas, quod mihi admodum displicebat.' The Latin poets of the ninth century are, in several cases, accused of the same tendency to outlandish diction. The style may have been started by chancery courts or some other state department; officialdom is always inclined to exalt its office by following the precept that language was invented to obscure thought, and if it should desire to inform the public that those who live in glass houses should not throw stones, it will state that 'individuals normally resident in dwelling-houses constructed wholly or mainly of glass or other vitreous substances should be careful to remember the potential repercussion consequent upon lapidary projection'.[1] Similar aberrations recur at other points of literary history; the rhétoriqueurs, the followers of Marini and Góngora, the burlesques, the précieux and the euphuists. If some of them have been the starting-point of new development, others have speedily disappeared, and are not without counterpart in our own times.[2]

A distinction can be made between *trobar ric* and *trobar clus*. Arnaut Daniel, the acknowledged representative of the former style, was an artist in vocabulary, metre and rime; an essential part of composition is described by him as 'filing and polishing'; the metaphor was not contradicted by Dante who described him as

> miglior fabbro del parlar materno.   (*Purg.* XXVI, 117.)

1 Cp.   'Cryptogamous concretion never grows
                On mineral fragments that decline repose.'
2 Metrical complexity and obscurity of diction are to be found in other early medieval literatures, such as Icelandic and Irish. It should not be assumed that the primitive is always the simple.

There is no great depth of thought in Arnaut Daniel's work; he was a technician, a medieval craftsman who enjoyed the exercise of his art as much as did the cathedral stone carvers, who were content to put their best efforts into work which might be placed almost out of sight but would make its contribution to the general effect. A stanza of 17 lines, the rimes of which did not find an answer until the succeeding stanzas were reached, while the rimes were of 'difficult' character, requiring wide search and ingenuity to find an adequate supply for five stanzas, such was the kind of problem which this troubadour preferred to attack. Obscurity was not his intention, and the difficulties which his poems present are those of vocabulary rather than of style.

Exponents of the *trobar clus* adopted the aristocratic standpoint; they considered that their art was degraded, if it could be intelligible to anyone without trouble and study; it was the poet's duty to regard and maintain it as an esoteric art, understood only by the initiated, somewhat in the spirit of the remark with which Dean Gaisford is reputed to have begun his divinity lecture: 'Gentlemen, a knowledge of Greek will enable you to read the oracles of God in the original and to look down from the heights of scholarship upon the vulgar herd, while leading occasionally to positions of considerable pecuniary emolument.' Thus Giraut de Bornelh, who for some time defended the obscure style, explained his position (ed. Kolsen, Halle, 1910, no. 26):

> Donc drechs es qu'eu chan
> C'a precs que per man;
> Mas era diran
> Que, si m'esforses
> Com levet chantes,
> Melhs m'ester' assatz.
> E non es vertatz;
> Que sens echartatz
> Adui pretz e.l dona
> ſi com l'ochaizona
> Nosens eslaissatz;
>   Mas be cre
> Que ges chans ancse
> No val al comensamen
> Tan com pois, can om l'enten.

'Then it is right for me to sing both to make my prayer and on account of
an order; but now people will say, that if I took trouble to sing in the light
style, it would be much better for me. And it is not true; for sense which is
remote (i.e. obscure) brings worth and grants it, even as unbridled stupidity
impairs it (i.e. obscure sense); but I certainly believe that no song is ever worth
as much at first, as it is later, when it is understood.'

Obscurity here is due to the use of words in strained senses (e.g.
echartatz, écarté) and to ambiguity of construction (e.g. does *l'ochaizona*
refer to *sens* or to *pretz*?). Further, we have a 15-line stanza, and pre-
cisely similar rimes have to be found for six more stanzas, the poem
being 'unissonans', which requirement is not likely to make for clarity.
Giraut explains his method as follows (no. 27):

> Mas, per melhs assire
> Mo chan,
> Vauc cerchan
> Bos motz en fre
> Que son tuch chargat e ple
> D'us estranhs sens naturals,
> E no sabon tuch de cals.

'But for the better foundation of my song I keep on the watch for words
good on the rein (i.e. tractable like horses) which are all loaded to the full (like
pack animals) and full of a meaning which is unusual and yet is wholly theirs;
but it is not everyone that knows what that meaning is.'

How much did the public understand of these alembicated compositions? Their impressions were auditory; could they hold in memory a
long sequence of rimes and anticipate in thought their repetition, while
attending also to the tune and the sense of the words? We get a hint
from an early passage in the *Razos de Trobar* of Raimon Vidal, that
there was literary and artistic hypocrisy in his time, as there is in ours.
'In this science of poetry both troubadours and hearers are often equally
deceived and I will tell you how and why. Hearers who understand
nothing, when they hear a good song, will pretend that they understand
very well because they think that they would be regarded as stupid,
if they said that they did not understand. Thus they deceive themselves,
for one of the most sensible things in the world is, if a man asks and
wishes to learn what he does not know, and the ignorant man has much
more reason for shame than the man who asks and wants to learn. And

those who do understand, when they hear a bad troubadour, will praise his song out of politeness; or if they do not praise it, at least they will not wish to condemn it. And thus the troubadours are deceived and the audience has the blame of it; for one of the best things in the world is, that a man praise what he ought to praise and condemn what he ought to condemn. Those who think that they understand and do not understand, from haughtiness do not learn and thus they remain deceived.' Raimon Vidal, in his didactic poem *Abrils issi' e mays intrava*, introduces a *joglar* who is unable to please the company which he finds in the courts of the nobles, and declares that his profession has been ruined by the general degradation of taste and culture and that he intends to abandon his profession. He asks Raimon for his advice. Raimon tells him that while culture (*saber e conoissenza*) is not entirely dead, a general lowering of taste is apparent; the *joglar* who wishes to succeed must therefore adapt his methods to his audience. This is not always an easy matter; 'I tell you that even among the worthy and excellent there are some who have no consideration; in a social gathering they will ask you to sing, and on the third word of your song, whatever it may be, they will begin to mutter and talk together quite close to you and exchange gossip. God never granted them understanding and, in my opinion, is never likely to grant it.'[1] This phenomenon is not unknown in modern society and it may be inferred that in the early years of the thirteenth century, when Raimon Vidal composed this poem, interest in the *trobar clus* was confined to narrow circles, and that even here, interest was not always genuine.

In any case, the *trobar clus* went out of fashion about the end of the twelfth century; the *trobar ric* was practised with varying success until the decline of Provençal poetry. Giraut de Bornelh was converted to the cause of *trobar clar* and in a *tenso* between himself and Linhaure (Raimbaut d'Aurenga) the arguments for either style are advanced.

(1) I should like to know, G. de Bornelh, why and for what reason you constantly blame the obscure style. Tell me whether you prize so highly that which is common to all? For then all would be equal.

(2) Sir Linhaure, I do not take it to heart if each man composes as he pleases; but judge that song to be more loved and prized which is made easy and simple, and do not be vexed at my opinion.

[1] Ed. W. Bohs, Erlangen, 1903, l. 1442.

(3) Guiraut, I do not like my songs to be so confused, that the base and the good, the small and the great be appraised alike; my poetry will never be praised by fools, for they have no understanding nor care for what is more precious and valuable.

(4) Linhaure, if I work late and turn my rest into weariness for that reason (to make my songs simple), does it seem that I am afraid of work? Why compose, if you do not want all to understand? Song brings no other advantage.

(5) Guiraut, provided that I produce what is best at all times, I care not if it be not so widespread; commonplaces are no good for the appreciative; that is why gold is more valued than salt, and with song it is even the same.

Thus one of the disputants believes that the object of writing poetry is to please a small circle of cultivated admirers by a display of technical skill; the other considers that the poet should have a message for the people and that even fools should be able to understand its purport. Giraut further insists that composition in the easy style demands no less skill and assiduity than is required for the production of obscurity. Upon this point he repeatedly insists: 'The troubadour who makes his meaning clear is just as clever as he who cunningly conjoins words.' 'My opinion is that it is not in obscure but in clear composition that toil is involved.' Raimon de Miraval, nearly contemporary in date (1168–1180), supported this view: 'Never should obscure poetry be praised, for it is composed only for a price, compared with sweet festal songs, easy to learn, such as I sing.' The Italian Lanfranc Cigala, at a later date (1241–1257), may have been moved to utterance by a recrudescence of obscure composition: 'I could easily compose an obscure, subtle poem, if I wished; but no poem should be so concealed beneath subtlety as not to be clear as day. For knowledge is of small value, if clearness does not bring light; obscurity has ever been regarded as death and brightness as life. And if anyone should lay this to my discredit or count it as foolishness in me, I know well that not four men in a thousand would agree with that view; and as I have so many on my side, I can indict him on the charge of folly; and it is great foolishness that composes obscure words, as if a man had profound wisdom who did not know enough to draw his water from a clear stream.'

Early in the thirteenth century a similar clash of critical opinion was heard in Germany, though the field of action was rather that of the court epic than of lyric poetry. Gotfrid von Strassburg is the champion of simplicity and clarity of style against the obscurity of Wolfram von

Eschenbach's composition; Gotfrid did not challenge his opponent by name, but few critics have doubted his identity to be proclaimed in Gotfrid's *Tristan* (ll. 4587–4818), where the poet expresses his views upon current poetical literature. After praising Hartmann von Aue for his clear and attractive style, he attacked Wolfram on two grounds: firstly, because he abandoned the accepted line of tradition in his narratives and went out of his way to introduce inventions of his own as a 'vindaere wilder maere', which, secondly, were made unintelligible by the complications of his style and the artificial character of his methods. The difference between the two men went deeper than questions of technique. Wolfram had an aristocratic audience in mind and an ideal of knightly chivalry before him; Gotfrid appealed rather to the citizen class and was concerned to attain an aesthetic rather than an ethical ideal; Gotfrid was concerned with Tristan's heart, Wolfram with Parzival's soul.[1]

These ideas were followed by Dante with certain modifications of his own. In the second book of the *De Vulgari Eloquentia*, he developed his theory of style. Having discovered the Illustrious Courtly Tongue, he discusses the subjects worthy of its use, and concludes that Arms, Love and Righteousness are the most worthy. The highest subjects should be sung in the highest style; while Dante accepts the theory of the three styles, which he calls Tragic, Comic and Elegiac, in place of *illustris, mediocris* and *humilis*, the choice of style is determined by the nature of the subject, and if the poet is to sing of the highest subjects, he must therefore use the tragic style. 'Stilo equidem tragico tunc uti videmur, quando cum gravitate sententie tam superbia carminum quam constructionis elatio et excellentia vocabulorum concordat'; 'We make use of the Tragic style when the stateliness of the lines as well as the loftiness of the construction and the excellence of the words agree with the weight of the subject', and this is therefore suitable for the *Canzone*, the highest form of poetry. Such is also the definition given in the *Leys d'Amors*,[2] which, if later in date than Dante's treatise, contains troubadour tradition on the subject. '*Chanso* should treat chiefly of love or praise, with fair pleasing words and gracious themes, for in a

---

1 On euphuism in England in the early fifteenth century, see *Florida Verborum Venustas*, by E. F. Jacob, in *Bulletin of the John Rylands Library*, vol. XVII, no. 2, July 1933.

2 Ed. Gatien-Arnoult, I, p. 339.

chanso should be set no low nor evil word nor any ill-chosen, for it should treat of love and praise, and a lover must show himself courteous not only in his acts, but likewise in his words and his speech.' On the question of construction suitable to the *canzone*, Dante shows obvious acquaintance with the treatises upon rhetoric; the example which he gives of the 'sapidus et venustus et excelsus' construction, 'Ejecta maxima parte florum, de sinu tuo, Florentia, nequicquam Trinacriam Totila secundus adivit', begins with an ablative absolute in inverted order, containing a 'conceit', apostrophises Florence and plays upon the names Florence and Totila, placing the names and the 'annominatio' in chiasmus, while the rule of the 'cursus' (cursus tardus to end the first clause, and cursus planus to close the whole phrase) is observed. These are tricks which the rhetoricians had fully analysed. When we come to the choice of words, Dante's knowledge of their works is even more obvious. He classifies words as *puerilia*, *muliebria* and *virilia*; the last mentioned are again divided as *silvestria* and *urbana*, and 'eorum que urbana vocamus quedam pexa et lubrica, quedam irsuta et reburra sentimus'; the *pexa* and *irsuta* are to be sought for use in the *canzone* as being *grandiosa*. These metaphors are concerned with personal appearance and in particular with the condition of the hair, or the surface of textile fabrics. To suggest that Dante had in mind the idea that words are a vesture of thought seems far-fetched, nor does the simile of the construction of a faggot (viii, 1; 'cantionem ligare', iv, 6) support it. There is some suggestion of a vesture simile in the last words of chapter 1; 'wherefore, since the theme of those who write verse always persists as an ingredient separate from the words, it will not, unless of the highest quality, appear better when associated with the best vulgar tongue, but worse, like an ugly woman, if dressed out in gold or silk'. But chapter 1 is a considerable distance from chapter vii. Dante is using metaphors which appear in the treatises upon versification and diction. Matthieu de Vendôme says (Faral, p. 154): 'ex superficiali ornatu verborum elegantia est in versibus.... Siquidem in hoc articulo versificatorem oportet esse expeditum, ne ex penuria ornatus hirsuta verborum aggregatio in metro videatur mendicare: sed, quadam similitudine sumpta a rebus materiatis, sicut de lana caprina et de panniculis inveteratis nemo festivum potest contexere indumentum... similiter in versibus.' Matthieu uses a variety of metaphorical expressions to describe the character of words, but returns more than once to those derived from outward appearance or clothing; *verba polita* are an essential element in verse; *quaedam dictiones panniculosae,* under which heading he places the conjunctions, are to be avoided. Geoffroi de Vinsauf follows the same line of thought (Faral, p. 254):

> Legibus arctetur metrum, sed prosa vagatur
> Liberiore via, quia prosae publica strata
> Admittit passim redas et plaustra; sed arta
> Semita versiculi non vult tam grossa, sed ipsas
> Voces in forma gracili, ne corpus agreste
> Verbi mole sua perturbet et inquinet illum
> Vultque venire metrum tanquam domicellula, compto
> Crine, nitente gena, subtili corpore, forma
> Egregia.

Dante's opposition of *verba silvestria* to *verba urbana,* and of *pexa* to *irsuta,* is here made. Geoffroi goes on to say that words must conform to these principles, 'nec quicquam puerile sonent', again using one of Dante's terms. He concludes this section of his poem thus:

> Ecce dedi pecten, quo si sint pexa relucent
> Carmina tam prosae quam metra. Sed an bene pectas
> Hoc speculo poteris plene discernere formam.

Evrard l'Allemand seems to use the same metaphor (p. 359):

> Persephones raptum qui compto carmine claudit,
> Arte nec ingenio claudicat ille suo.

He wrote in 1349, too late to concern us; by that time the idea had probably become commonplace; Góngora uses it (*Sonetos Heroicos,* no. XXI):

> Historia es culta, cuyo encanecido
> Estilo, si no métrico, peinado,
> Tres ya Pilotos del bajel sagrado
> Hurta al tiempo....

These metaphors were no doubt suggested by some association of ideas, too elusive to be recovered by us. No word which has a meaning for speaker or hearer is ever entirely isolated; its utterance arouses associations which are usually wholly personal, and, if analysed, may appear to be entirely irrational. Nor is the problem made easier by the difficulty of determining how far the auditory impression by which associations were evoked was disturbed by visual reminiscences. In any case the choice of words was as important to the rhetoricians as to the writers of classical French tragedy; the difference between *mots sénateurs* and *mots roturiers* was fully recognised:

> Florida vernabunt, fabri arte polita micabunt,
> Pulchra quidem mulier formosa sit et speciosa,
> Aurum sit purum, sit mundum, sit rubicundum.

> (Faral, p. 105.)

Boccaccio and his friend Petrarch defended the obscurity of poetry as both inevitable and useful. 'Surely no one can believe that poets invidiously veil the truth with fiction, either to deprive the reader of the hidden sense, or to appear the more clever; but rather to make truths, which would otherwise grow cheap by exposure, the object of strong intellectual effort and various interpretation, that in ultimate discovery they shall be more precious.' ... 'In poetic narrative, above all, the poets maintain majesty of style and corresponding dignity. As saith Francis Petrarch in the Third Book of his *Invectives*, "such majesty and dignity are not intended to hinder those who wish to understand, but rather propose a delightful task, and are designed to enhance the reader's pleasure and to support his memory. What we acquire with difficulty and keep with care is always the dearer to us."' ... 'I repeat my advice to those who would appreciate poetry and unwind its difficult involutions. You must read, you must persevere, you must inquire and exert the utmost power of your mind. If one way does not lead to the desired meaning, take another; until, if your strength holds out, you will find that clear which at first looked dark.'[1]

Dante's critical faculty has been doubted by various writers. Macaulay, for instance, in his essay on Dante, says, 'it is impossible not to remark Dante's admiration of writers far inferior to himself, and in particular, his idolatry of Virgil, who, elegant and splendid as he is, has no pretensions to the depth and originality of mind which characterise his Tuscan worshipper. In truth, it may be laid down as an almost universal rule, that good poets are bad critics'. Certainly, Dante's reference to Cicero, Livy, Pliny, Frontinus and Orosius, without a breath of discrimination, as writers 'qui usi sunt altissimas prosas', suggests that his criterion of excellence was not the same as ours. His ideal figure among

1 C. G. Osgood, *Boccaccio on Poetry*, Princeton, 1930, pp. 60 ff.

the troubadours is Arnaut Daniel, an artist in words and metres, with which means he adorns the commonest of commonplaces. Of the few troubadours who struck the real lyric note of emotion, Bernart de Ventadorn is outstanding; he has been styled, with some justification, the troubadour Wordsworth; of him Dante has nowhere a word to say. Yet he almost repeats Bernart's description of real poetry:

> Io mi son un che, quando
> Amore spira, noto, e in quel modo
> Ch'ei detta dentro, vo significando.   (*Purg.* xxiv, 52.)

This is not essentially different from Bernart (ed. Appel, no. 15):

> Chantars no pot gaire valer,
> si d'ins dal cor no mou lo chans;
> ni chans no pot dal cor mover,
> si no i es fin' amors coraus;
> per so es mos chantars cabaus
> qu'en joi d'amor ai et enten
> la boch' e.ls olhs e.l cor e.l sen.

'Song can be of little value, if it rises not from the depths of the heart; and song cannot spring from the heart, if there is not there pure heartfelt love. For that reason my song is supreme, for I have and hold in the transport of love my mouth and eyes and heart and sense.'

Modern criticism naturally asks, why choose the artificial when the natural is available?

There are many passages in the *Divina Commedia* which are obscure to any understanding, and others which are grotesque to modern taste; J. A. Symonds has discussed some of them in his *Introduction to the Study of Dante*. The truth seems to be, that Dante never entirely broke away from medieval ideas upon the nature of style and the use of language; Giraut de Bornelh abandoned the *trobar clus* and gained a reputation in the clear and easy style; for that reason Dante places him below Arnaut Daniel, whom he regards as a poet of supreme excellence, because he had treated the highest possible subject, love, in the most elevated of all possible styles. There is, however, this wide difference between Dante and the troubadours; they used the obscure style to impress their audience; Dante used it to 'ennoble' his subject, that is, to secure for it a greater measure of authority and dignity. Moreover, Dante was a pioneer; he was using a language that was still hardly formed to deal with the most profound and complicated theological and metaphysical questions. But when he forgets the rules and follows his own inspiration, there are few greater poets than he.

Dante was no lover of stylistic affectation for its own sake. In the *Convivio* (I, x), when defending the use of the vernacular in place of Latin, he is one of the first in medieval times to place a right value upon prose as a medium of expression. 'By the help of this commentary, the great excellence of the vulgar tongue will be seen, because not only are the loftiest and newest conceptions almost as suitably, adequately and gracefully expressed by it as by Latin itself, but its virtues cannot be fully displayed in rimed compositions on account of the incidental adornments which are linked with them; I mean time and rhythm and ordered numbers; just as with the beauty of a lady, when the decoration of her ornaments and apparel attracts more admiration for her than her person itself.' If the full resources inherent in a language are to be known, they will be best displayed in prose, where adventitious ornament will not distract attention from its fundamental qualities. In this matter, Dante is in advance, not only of his own age, but also of Petrarch. Conversely (*ibid.* I, vii), 'let everyone know that nothing which is harmoniously compacted by the bond of the Muse can be translated from its own language to another without destroying its sweetness and harmony. And this is the reason why Homer has not been translated from Greek into Latin like the other writings which the Greeks have bequeathed to us; and this is the reason why the verses of the Psalter have none of the sweetness and music of harmony, for they were translated from Hebrew into Greek and from Greek into Latin, and in the first translation all that sweetness disappeared.' The success or even the possibility of translation depends upon the subject-matter; in the case of poetry, where the highest form must correspond with the loftiness of the subject, translation can, at most, substitute something different from the original.

These were new ideas, which came to modify and supplement the rules and recommendations of the rhetoricians. They had written with the demands and requirements of oratory at the back of their minds, having in view a public which would listen, but could not read. Dante is aware that another public was beginning to exist, a public which would read to itself, for information, reflection and pleasure.

M. Faral, in the preface to his *Recherches sur les Sources latines des Contes et Romans Courtois du Moyen Age* (Paris, 1913) draws an interesting contrast between the knowledge of the Latin classical works possessed respectively by medieval writers and by the members of the Pléiade; the men of 1150 he considers, and with justice, to have been as well informed upon this literature as the men of 1550. The difference between them was a matter of quality, not of degree, of manner, not of matter. 'Ce que les écrivains de la Pléiade ont apporté de neuf, ce n'a pas été une connaissance plus étendue, mais une conception inédite de la littérature romaine. Ils ont abordé l'étude des poètes anciens aved une autre âme, une autre sensibilité et une autre imagination qu'on ne l'avait fait jusque-là; et c'est dans la nouveauté de l'interprétation qu'a consisté leur véritable originalité. De la renaissance poétique du XVIe siècle, l'agent principal n'a pas été la révélation des textes antiques, mais une intelligence nouvelle de leur sens.... Tout en admettant l'existence, au XIIe siècle, d'une puissante tradition antique, on n'oubliera pas que, dans la production littéraire de ce temps, l'esprit selon lequel on a lu les textes conservés a eu autant d'importance, sinon plus, que le fait même qu'ils étaient lus.'

This difference, which M. Faral was not concerned to analyse further, is that which divides the age of script from the age of print, the age of auditory from that of visual comprehension. Authors of 1150 wrote works intended primarily for recitation; those of 1550 wrote for a public that could read as well as listen. In the age of print, the reader has time to ponder the matter before him, to read a passage over as often as he pleases and to exert his critical faculties. For him, words have a wider connotation than for the hearer and a new significance derived from their juxtaposition with other words and from their position in the sentence or phrase. The case is well illustrated by the works, the origins of which M. Faral has investigated. Virgil was a literary artist whose work may well have been recited, but was intended to be read; full appreciation of his delicate art would never be acquired by one or even several hearings. In some respects his style is not only personal, but remarkably modern. Consider, for instance, his use of 'le mot évocateur', the word or phrase that intensifies a picture by provoking associated ideas. The first pages of the *Aeneid* will provide examples. After the shipwreck off the African coast, a fire is lighted (l. 175):

> Ac primum silici scintillam excudit Achates
> Suscepitque ignem foliis atque arida circum
> Nutrimenta dedit rapuitque in fomite flammam.

'Suscipere' denotes the act by which a father acknowledged paternity when he took his new-born child in his arms for the first time; and the description of Achates crouching over the new-born spark and keeping it alive is heightened by contrast with the domestic scene suggested, the young father, careful not to drop the precious infant and conscious of his duty for its future support, for which must be provided no 'arida nutrimenta'. The author of the twelfth-century *Eneas*,[1] who had certainly read Virgil in the text, was content to state baldly,

> Les feus alument el gravier,
> si apresterent lo mangier. (l. 229.)

Or again, when the other shipwrecked party made their way to Carthage headed by Ilioneus and pleaded their case before Dido in her palace,

> Tum breviter Dido, voltum demissa, profatur.

The phrase has been misinterpreted by some commentators, who explain the action as due to modesty, not a prominent feature in Dido's character. After the speech of Ilioneus, Virgil wished to recall the scene to his readers in the detail previously described. Dido is seated 'high on a throne of royal state which far Outshone the wealth of Ormuz or of Ind',

> saepta armis, solioque alte subnixa resedit. (l. 506.)

She has therefore to 'look down' upon the ragged band of mariners standing before the throne, and the action helps the reader to visualise the scene. The French poet simply cut it out:

> Dido respondi al mesage: (l. 599.)

In this manner he destroyed the life and colour of the poem and left what we regard as dry bones. But he could do no other; touches of the kind discussed had no interest or appeal for his audience who wanted

1 Ed. Salverda de Grave, *Les Classiques français du Moyen Age,* 2 vols. Paris, 1925.

merely a story of adventure, with rapid movement, plenty of incident and a love interest.

So we are brought to the conclusion that style, in our modern sense of the term, does not come to recognition until social changes have produced a reading and not a hearing public. Not until education had made reading a pastime and the invention of printing had begun to stabilise orthography and grammar was it possible for an author to develop and a reader to recognise that personal touch which is the basis of an individual style. When auditory are replaced by visual impressions,[1] when it becomes possible to read and read again a page of matter, when words begin to collect associations and to have a wider connotation than the merely spoken word can acquire, then the stylist begins to emerge from the common herd and to rise above the mechanical precepts of the rhetoricians. The question is sometimes asked, when did the middle ages come to an end? They ended, so far as their idea of literary style is concerned, with the invention of printing.

[1] Horace, *De Arte Poetica*, l. 180, though referring to the stage, is appropriate here:

> Segnius irritant animos demissa per aurem
> Quam quae sunt oculis subjecta fidelibus...

Cp. Cicero, *De Oratore* III, 41, 163: 'facilius ad ea, quae visa, quam ad illa quae audita sunt, mentis oculi feruntur'. Herodotus, I, 8 (the story of Candaules and Gyges): ὦτα γὰρ τυγχάνει ἀνθρώποισι ἐόντα ἀπιστότερα ὀφθαλμῶν.

CHAPTER V

PROSE & TRANSLATION

UNTIL the end of the twelfth century literature produced for public entertainment or edification was almost entirely written in verse. The earliest specimens of French prose are legal documents, such as the Laws of William the Conqueror, or translations of the Bible. Prose made its way by slow degrees, as education advanced and as people learned to read for themselves; prose versions of earlier poems began to appear at the end of the twelfth century to meet the taste of readers who wanted a story devoid of the padding and prolixity which delayed the action in the verse narratives. The story-teller who told his tales in prose was also a figure in social amusement, whether he was a professional (*conteor*) or an amateur who volunteered to amuse a company at a loss for occupation, and may have helped to introduce a taste for prose romances and short stories. The prose version of Robert de Boron's *Joseph of Arimathea*, to which his *Merlin* was added, is the earliest considerable work of the kind known to us. Then came the prose versions of the Tristan story, which was known to Brunetto Latini, and of the Arthurian romances. Much of this increasing amount of prose writing was in the form of translation; Philippe de Dreux, for instance, translated among other works the Latin pseudo-Turpin in 1206 for Count Renaut of Boulogne, who commissioned a prose translation on the ground that verse could not be sufficiently literal. When Ville-hardouin produced his *Conquête de Constantinople* about 1213, prose writing may be said to have fairly started on its career.

Villehardouin was the first of a series of chroniclers who helped to satisfy curiosity concerning the crusades and the lands in which they were fought. There was also a desire for more information upon the history of the past. The historical information at the disposal of even the cultivated classes must have been singularly scanty and inaccurate, so long as they were dependent upon the works of Wace, Benoît de Sainte-Maure and others of the kind, while the information to be derived from the *chansons de geste* and the *chansons d'aventure* with their fantastic geography and wild anachronisms must have induced the inquirer to form a historical perspective no less surprising than the zoological information provided by the *bestiaires*. Yet there were valuable chronicles to be found, if anyone had cared to translate them from the Latin of their monastic authors. Consider the many volumes of the Rolls Series in this country, the Monumenta Germaniae Historiae, the numerous chronicles and annals produced and preserved in such great abbeys as those of Saint-Benoît-sur-Loire, Saint-Remy-de-Reims, and such writers as Suger, Richer and others who had recorded the annals of the past, and we shall be astonished at the lack of curiosity which allowed these writings to remain untranslated for centuries in the obscurity of their monastic Latin. The Normans in this country and on the continent had certainly shown an interest in history for family and personal reasons; a typical case is the life in verse of William the Marshal, composed by a minstrel who was commissioned to produce the narrative and was provided by the family with the necessary information. But the most cultivated of Frenchmen in the time of Louis VII or of Philippe Auguste must have known singularly little of French history, and the spread of enlightenment, even during the thirteenth century, was by no means rapid. The Anonyme de Béthune made a start about 1225 with translations of the pseudo-Turpin and the *Historia Regum Francorum*, after which little was done until 1274 when *Les Grandes Chroniques de France* began to emerge from the Abbey of Saint-Denis. Between 1260 and 1270 was compiled a collection of historical anecdotes, known by the title conferred by their editor as *Récits d'un Ménestrel de Reims*; their style suggests that the author was a professional *conteor* who here put together some part of the material which he used for recitation and which included such unhistorical matter as Queen Eleanor's relations with Saladin, the captivity of Richard Cœur de Lion and his discovery by Blondel.

The twelfth century had been the age of romance; the thirteenth was the age of reason. Education was rapidly increasing; thousands of students, belonging chiefly to the lower classes, flocked to the universities and especially to Paris, and the system of instruction which made disputation its object naturally stimulated the spirit of inquiry. The demand for books and the desire to read them in French, rather than in crabbed Latin, set translators to work; a complete version of the Bible appeared in Paris about 1235, probably with the countenance of the university. The *Corpus Juris* and the *Codex* of Justinian were also translated.

Theological controversy at this time was keen and often acrimonious; Augustinians disputed with Aristotelians, Thomists with Averroists, and shook the bases of traditional authority with their continual polemics; Roger Bacon propounded his 'experimental' method. Writers began to express views upon current affairs and social conditions. Constitutional changes of great importance were also in progress: the growing power and influence of the crown restricted the independence of both the feudal nobility and of the towns; the legislative and administrative functions of government were separated and the *Parlement* as a judicial body became more and more influential. Hence the importance attached to the study of canon law at Paris and Montpellier. With and because of these changes, the several social classes became less departmental or parochial and began to think of their position as related to the crown rather than as subject to an overlord. The resulting spirit of criticism was reflected in literature, the outstanding features of which are twofold: satirical writing of the kind to be found in the *Roman de Renart* and the *Roman de la Rose*, or in the writings of those, such as Rutebœuf, who considered that change was another name for degeneracy; and the relation of contemporary events by realistic observers. Villehardouin and his successors were neither satirists nor critics; they related as accurately as they could what they had seen or heard, and began to develop the art of description upon new lines.

All this gave a new stimulus to the writing of prose. It was seen that prose allowed a writer to give attention to the subject in hand without the distraction of hunting for rimes and other forms of decoration or padding. Prose became distinguished as dealing with matters of fact and not of fancy; it was a scientific medium. Therefore, to tell a story in prose was to invest it with an air of realism which verse dissipated in the first few couplets; it became clear that a family chronicle, written in verse, would vastly gain in authority and dignity, if it were rewritten in prose; it would, in fact, become real history. Readers began to discover that the action of a story moved more quickly in prose than in poetry and a demand for prose narratives began as the taste for individual reading increased:

> Et elle, par sa courtoisie,
> Me dist: 'Jones homs, je vous prie
> Qu'un rommanc me prestes pour lire.
> Bien vees, ne vous le fault dire,

> Que je m'i esbas volontiers,
> Car lires est un douls mestiers,
> Quiconques le fait par plaisance.'
>
> (Froissart, *L'Espinette Amoureuse*, l. 845.)

The *Roman de Troie* of Benoît de Sainte-Maure appeared in prose as early as the middle of the thirteenth century. The epilogue to this version is as follows (*Roman de Troie*, ed. L. Constans, A.T.F. vol. VI, p. 268): 'Si vos ai ore menee a fin la vraie estoire de Troie, selonc ce que ele fu trovee escritte en l'almaire de Saint Pol de Corrinte en grezois langage, et dou grezois fu mise en latin, et ge la translatai en françois, non pas par rimes ne par vers, o il covient par fine force avoir maintes mençognes, com font ces menestriers qui de lor lengue font maintes fois rois et amis solacier, de quoi il font sovent lor profit et autrui doumage, mais par droit conte, selon ce que ge la trovai, sanz rien covrir de verité ne de mençogne demoustrer, en tel mainiere que nus ne poroit riens ajoindre ne mermer que por veraie deüst estre tenue.' The *remanieur* begins by ascribing an imaginary origin to his work, in order to enhance its authority. When he states that prose does not tell lies in the manner of the compositions of minstrels, he is merely stating the fact that epic poetry is associated in the mind of the·public with wonders and adventures outside of ordinary human experience, and that this is not expected of a prose composition, a medieval mode of asserting that prose is more 'realistic' than verse.

The *Roman du Comte d'Anjou*,[1] composed by Jehan Maillart in 1316, defines realism in the same manner. After speaking with some scorn of those who can be entertained only by fabulous *romans d'aventure*, which do nothing

> Fors que l'annui des cuers enchacent
> Par leurs contes et par leurs fables,

he proposes to tell a story which will have a moral purpose,

> Et qui lez cuers des genz esmeuvent
> A bien fere, quant il lez treuvent,
> Plus deligemment escouter
> Pour soi en bonnes meurs monter.
>
> . . . .

---

1 Ed. Mario Roques, *Les Classiques français du moyen âge*, Paris, 1931.

Pour ce m'est il volenté prise
Que je vous conpte et vous devise,
En lieu de mençonge et de fable,
Une aventure veritable.

It will keep within the limits of human experience and will be told in
rime, as that gives pleasure. Realism is attempted not only by avoidance
of the miraculous, but by catalogues and descriptions of dress, furniture
and other technical matters, by details of a bedroom scene after a
wedding, and by the introduction or mention of such details as
'corner l'iaue', before dinner (l. 2364), upon which signal the guests
washed their hands before entering the dining-hall. All this is in line
with the ideas of the *prosificateur* of the *Roman de Troie*, with the exception of the use of verse.

The whole process is illustrated by the history of the French national
epic, the history of its transformation from assonant verse to prose. The
spirit of reverence with which these early monuments of literature had
been regarded was slowly undermined by the advance of education;
the exploits which they chronicled were examined with eyes increasingly
sceptical, which saw no reason why impious hands should not be laid
upon the epic. Moreover, ears had grown accustomed to full rime
under the influence of lyric poetry, and eyes which had begun to read
instinctively expected coincidence of sound to be repeated in script.
The early methods of sung or chanted recitation were superseded by
the practice of reading aloud; entertainment was not dependent upon
the services of a professional jongleur; the amateur reader could display
his accomplishment to any chance gathering of hearers and the jingle
of rime was preferred to the less obvious harmony of assonance. Jehan
Maillart says that he undertook the task at the request of a 'grant sires
en la court de France', and states that the audience which he had in view
regarded rime as indispensable:

Et je, pour sa volenté faire
Et que cil qui l'orront retraire
Pour la biauté et l'acordance
De la rime i truissent plesance,
Me sui je voulu entremettre
De l'aventure en rime mettre.

The *rajeunisseur* or *remanieur* was confronted by the difficulty that
assonant words could not always be made to rime, even when replaced

by synonyms. Hence he was obliged to paraphrase, to place intractable words in the interior of the line, and to use various forms of padding and set formulae to secure his rime sequence. The long alexandrine did not relieve him of this difficulty, which was increased by the use of octosyllabic verse, with the result that rimed versions are considerably longer than the assonanced originals. The _remanieur_ did not scruple to suppress parts of the original and to add incidents drawn from his own imagination or from other sources. So the epic character of the poem disappeared; it became a _roman d'aventure_, vigorous and readable in the hands of such a master as Chrétien de Troyes, but utterly monotonous when produced by a mediocre rhymester. Then came the demand for stories in prose and the _dérimeur_ was ready to supply it.

The authors of these prose versions often feel obliged to apologise for their procedure or to explain it; in the North of France the taste for verse appears to have continued after the appearance of prose versions elsewhere, and prose authors were sensible of the fact that they were innovators. The author of the prose _Chevalier au Cygne_ in the thirteenth century said: 'j'ai commanchie sans rime pour l'estore avoir plus abregiee. Et si me sanle que la rime est moult plaisans et moult bele; mais moult est longue'. The anonymous author of an enormous compilation dealing with the history of Charles Martel and Pepin, which was concluded in 1448, said that he wrote in prose 'pour ce que aujourd'hui les grans princes et autres seigneurs appetent plus la prose que la ryme, et pour le langaige quy est plus entier et n'est mie constraint'.[1] The epic poems which formed the cycle of Guillaume d'Orange were utilised in the fifteenth century by the author of the long prose romance under the same title; it may have been composed for Jacques d'Armagnac, Duc de Nemours, who was beheaded in 1477. Two versions of this work are extant, a fact which suggests that it was not unpopular. To form this compilation, the author condensed the matter of thirteen _chansons de geste_. The first of those thus treated, the prose version of _Aimeri de Narbonne_ begins: 'qui d'armes, d'amours, de noblesse et de chevalerie vouldra ouïr beaux mots et plaisans raconter, mette paine et face silence, ou lise qui lire vouldra, et il pourra savoir et aprendre comment Aimeri de Beaulande conquist la cité de Narbonne', and states that the adaptor has 'translaté de vielle rime en telle prose, car plus volentiers s'esbat l'en maintenant qu'on ne souloit,

1 P. Meyer, Introduction to _Girart de Roussillon_, Paris, 1884, p. clix.

et plus est le langage plaisant prose que rime; ce dient ceulx aux quieulx il plaist et qui ainsi le veulent avoir'.[1] There was thus a definite demand for prose, beginning in the thirteenth century and increasing continuously. Education, as we have said, increased the number of those who could read for their own amusement or who were able by reading aloud to amuse their friends. Readers were bored by rhetorical devices intended to show the capacity of a minstrel or reciter and by the stock epithet, the *chevilles* and the turns of expression to which composers were driven in their search for rimes; they wanted incident and plot.

In Spain and Portugal a similar order of development is apparent; verse precedes prose, which is called into being by increasing interest in history and the spread of education and culture, which demanded information in a vernacular tongue. Catalan has been regarded as exceptional among Romance literatures, in that its beginnings are in prose and not in verse; the chronicle of James the Conqueror and the chronicles of Desclot, Muntaner and Pedro IV will bear comparison with the work of any chronicler in Western Europe. Though the chronicle of James was not published until some 150 years after its composition, his example and his energy in causing translations to be made encouraged secular writers to use their own tongue; when James had shown the way, Ramon Lull set Catalan prose upon a firm footing and showed other writers how excellent an instrument they had in hand. If these prose writers are regarded as the founders of literary Catalan, the fact must not be forgotten that the field of poetry had been occupied by troubadour productions years before the chronicle of James was produced; Provençal examples were constantly imitated by writers south of the Pyrenees and similarity of language is so close that it is sometimes difficult to say where Catalan begins and Provençal ends. Hence Catalan cannot be regarded as an exception to the general line of development. This thirteenth-century movement continued concurrently in Castile under the influence of Alfonso X, el Sabio, whose

1 A.T.F. vol.1, pp. ccxlvii ff. The earliest MS. of this version is of the fifteenth century, but the version itself probably belongs to the fourteenth century. See also P. Henry, *Les Enfances Guillaume*, A.T.F. 1935, p. xxxviii. *Translater* in this connection has a wider meaning than our 'translate'. It may denote compilation, adaptation, paraphrase, etc., in short, transference, as the original word implies. For examples in Middle English, see F. R. Amos, *Early Theories of Translation*, New York, 1920.

immense scientific and legal work was crowned by the historical writing which he set on foot, in particular, the *General Historia* and the *Primera Crónica General*. The latter work, which concerned the history of Spain, incorporated the narratives provided by epic poetry; the Spanish *juglares* treated subjects approximating in date to their own times, whereas French epic dealt with remoter and more general themes. The *Poema del Cid* is an historical narrative of regional character, based upon facts of history and geography, in contrast to the vague historical perspective of an epic from the Charlemagne or Breton cycles. The *Crónica General* refers to these epics without naming them individually; 'algunos dizen en sus cantares et en sus fablas de gesta'. The admirable researches of Ramón Menéndez Pidal have raised some, at least, of these shadowy figures from obscurity. In Portugal, again, lyric poetry preceded prose, which did not become a literary instrument until the fourteenth century was well advanced; the fragments classified as epic which have come down to us do not suggest that Portugal or Galicia produced anything in the nature of an epic school. Probably French influence penetrating along the road to Compostela made native epic superfluous; the existence of a fourteenth-century Galician prose version of Benoît de Sainte-Maure's *Roman de Troie* suggests that the Galician reader was satisfied with French art, so far as epic was concerned.

The social and political changes which stimulated the fashion of prose writing in Germany show a certain outward similarity to the course of development which gave prose its importance in French literature. Middle High German literature until about 1250 consisted almost entirely of verse, romance, lyric and satire; prose was confined to the exposition of ecclesiastical and legal concerns. But with the close of the crusades, the introduction of new methods of warfare, resulting from the invention of gunpowder, deprived the old-style knight of much of his military importance. The rise of the towns to wealth and power produced a new class of merchant citizens, able to rival the domination of the knightly families and possessed of social ideals which were by no means within the noble and courtly categories. Thus the knightly classes sank in the social scale and the weaker of them became little better than brigands or freebooters. Town society, whatever virtues it had, was not appreciative of codes of chivalry nor of upper-class polish and culture; if it wished to hear the old stories of adventure and prowess, all it desired was the narrative, and clumsy prose or jingling doggerel was considered an adequate medium for this purpose. Thus, with the fifteenth century the age of prose began, and, as in France, the medieval verse epic was superseded by the prose romance, and by a mass of anecdotal and satirical compositions in which wit was replaced by the buffoonery and 'slap-stick' comedy which has at all times been dear to the German middle-class mind.

The process of turning verse into prose is not without interest. The simple method was to destroy rime and rhythm by changing words, altering or omitting conventional set phrases and other devices for securing a rime at need, paraphrasing doubtful passages, while keeping the language of the original so far as this could be done without betraying the fact that the original was in verse. Consider the opening lines of Fouke Fitzwarin (1268):

En le temps de Averil e May quant les prees e les herbes reverdissent e chescune chose vivaunte recovre vertue, beaute e force, les mountz e les valeys retentissent des douces chauntz des oseylouns e les cuers de chescune gent pur la beaute du temps e la sesone mountent en haut e s'en jolyvent, donque deit home remembrer des aventures e pruesses nos auncestres qe se penerent pur honour en leauté quere e de teles choses parler qe a plusours purra valer.

Seygnours, vous avez oy eynz ces houres qe William Bastard duc de Normaundie vynt ou grant gent e pueple santz nounbre en engleterre....

The conventional opening of the beauty of spring and its effects upon the mind, together with the fact that the beginning of the narrative is an appeal to listeners, not to readers, is enough to arouse suspicion. Octosyllabic lines become obvious at the first reading:

> Quant pres et herbes reverdissent
> E mountz e valeys retentissent
> Des douces chauntz des oseylouns,
> Par la beaute de la sesoun,
> E les cuers en haut mountent
> De chescune gent et s'en jolyvent,
> Donque deit home remembrer
> Les pruesses nos auncestres
> E de teles choses parler
> Que a plusours purront valer.

It is not easy to keep poetry out of sight in the task of prosification. Molière left alexandrines and half-alexandrines in *L'Avare*, for reasons which do not here concern us. But it was especially difficult for the medieval *remanieur*, who was hampered by his powerful memory in divesting his thoughts of the original verse. Here is a case where the *remanieur* failed completely and apparently gave up the attempt in despair (Wright, *Political Songs and Poems*, Rolls Series, II, pp. 124 f.). It is a contemporary poem on the battle of Agincourt (1415), which the writer of an early chronicle of London was attempting to utilise. King Henry is addressing his army:

'Allso, archers, to yow I praye, no fote that ye flee away, erste we be alle beten in this felde. And thenke be Englysshemen that never wold fle at no batelle, for agenste one of us thowthe ther be tene, thenke Criste wil help us in owre right. Bot I wold no blode wer spilte, Cryste helpe me so now in this case, but tho that been cause of this trespase; when thou sittest in jugment, ther holde me excused tofore thi face, as thou art God omnipotent. But passe we all now in fere, duke, erle and bachelere, of all owre synnys he make us sekere. Jentil Jesus, borne of Marye, and as for us thou deydyst on good Fryday, as thi will was, so brynge us to thi blisse an hy, and graunte us ther to have a place. Do and bete on ffaste,' owre kynge tho bad wythe fulle glad chere; and so thei dyde at that word, lord, knyght and archere. Ther men myght see a semble sade that turnyd many onto tene and tray, for many a lorde ther ryght low lay that commen was of blod full gent. By evensong tyme sothely to say, ther help us God omnipotent.

> Stedes ther stumbleyd in that stownde,
>   That stod stere stuffed under stele;
> With gronyng grete thei felle to grownde,
>   Here sydes federed whan thei gone fele.
>   Owre lord the kynge he foght ryght wele,
> Scharpliche on hem his spere he spent,
>   Many on seke he made that sele,
> Thorow myght of God omnipotent.

The last two words form a refrain for each stanza; seven more follow. It seems to have dawned upon the compiler of the last of the lines printed as prose (they are here printed as they appear in the MS.) that in attempting to paraphrase he was merely repeating the poem, which he then determined to finish without further alteration. Wright quotes a similar case on p. xxx of his introduction to the volume in which this poem appears, when a chronicler attempted to work a ballad into his prose narrative and abandoned the paraphrase for the original. In these cases, it is not necessary to suppose that the writer of the prose version had the verse text before him; he probably knew it by heart and was too completely dominated by the original to be able to reduce it to prose.

Some verse compositions may have been gradually reduced to prose by recitation on the part of incompetent performers who had little ear for poetry and were painfully anxious to secure that their hearers should understand the text; in the interests of this purpose, they were inclined to gloss or paraphrase the original. The introduction to *Lo Novel Sermon*, one of the Vaudois poems, is as follows:[1]

> Li legent aquest novel sermon entendan sanament
> Car yo non l'ay script per necessita de scriptura qu'el en fos mancament
> Ni per despreci del noo ni del velh testament,
> Ni per alcun doctor endendent sanament,
> Mas per la grossa e per la simpla gent.
> Mas tot se pon provar ço que es script en aquest novel sermon
> Per sapiencia divina o per clara raçon.
> Enperço yo l'apello lo certan serviment,
> Car, facent ço qu'el di, e gardant nos de ço qu'ilh nos defent,
> Servent a dio entro a la fin, il trobaren salvament.

The metre of this poem is in twelve-syllable lines in *laisses* of unequal length, broken by many irregularities which suggest a process of oral transmission by reciters who were more anxious to instil sound doctrine than to observe the requirements of metre. In l. 2 *en* was misunderstood and *per necessita* was added as an explanation, after which *ni* was prefixed to the next line to connect it with the foregoing. Similarly, l. 9 was enlarged to explain the sense of the first half; the second half was thrust out of place, and an attempt was made to construct an extra half line to precede it. A little more tinkering and a scribe to write it continuously as prose in order to save parchment, and we should have a version that could be regarded as prose. The original may have run thus:

> Li legent mio sermon, entendan sanament
> Que non l'ay script per ço qu'el en fos mancament,
> Per despreci del noo ni del velh testament,
> Ni per alcun doctor entendent sanament,
> Mas per lo grosier poble e per la simpla gent.

1 *Six Vaudois Poems*, Cambridge University Press, p. 16. This introduction is given in one only of the three MSS.

Mas tot se po provar ço qu'es en lo sermon
Per sapiença divina ɔ per clara raçon.
Enperço l'apello lo certan serviment,
Car, facent ço qu'el di, trobaren salvament.

Bérinus[1] is a lengthy prose *roman d'aventure* which has attracted the
attention of folk-lore researchers, as it introduces stories taken from
widely different sources; the adventures of Sinbad the Sailor, the treasure
of Rhampsinitus, the Seven Sages of Rome, and other oriental tales are
laid under contribution to provide a rapid series of events. It seems to
have enjoyed some popularity, as four MS. versions exist, four early
printed copies and a middle English version, the *Tale of Beryn*, for some
time attributed to Chaucer. The discovery of two fragments in verse
proved, what had been already suspected, that the prose version was
not original. The two fragments are not from the same MS., and as
they are all that now survives of the original verse, it may not be rash
to conclude that the verse was not highly esteemed. The prologue
which appeals to 'tous ceulx qui mon livre orront' ('orront ou liront'
in two MSS.) says that 'la matiere est delitable a oyr et proufitable a
retenir, sy ay grant merveille que li bon trouveour qui jadiz furent n'en
ont fait plus grant mencion et mise en plus grant auctorite'. Regrets
follow concerning the decay of minstrelsy owing to the neglect of the
nobility and the decay of 'joye et courtoisie'. It is likely that the
remanieur, whose work is dated 1350–70, is here reproducing the original
matter; octosyllabic lines can be seen in the passage just quoted. He
appears to have had in view a public which was not greatly interested
in 'la courtoisie' and much that the term implied; an analysis of the
nature and effects of love is cut short; detailed descriptions of combats
and ceremonies are summarised, with the object of maintaining rapidity
of action and of suppressing the various devices, the circumlocutions
and padding which the jongleur used in the interests of rime. Otherwise, he follows the original pretty closely and does not hesitate to
repeat it almost verbatim. The following extract will indicate his
procedure. Aigres meets a messenger summoning him to Rome:

Co fu un jor de Seint Denise,   (Par. 546) Or dist le compte que tout
Kant li estez de yver devise   droit le jour Saint Denis, a l'issue
E d'esté chiet la grant chalour,   d'esté
E li tens tret vers la freour,

1 *Anciens Textes français*, par R. Bossuat, Paris, 1931.

Ke Aygres issi de Dijon,   5

Od lui Orchas son compaignon;

Esbanoiant desor Morel,

S'en vait par devant le chastel,

Tant qu'il voient, par aventure,

Venir vers els grant aleüre   10

Un message mult travaillé,

Ki de errer out le front moillé.

Einsint com Fortune li meine,

Ke tot le monde a en demeine,

En vient vers les dous barons droit.

'Amis, dunt viens tu orendroit'?   16

Fait Aigres, qui primer l'apele,

'Si tu sez alcune novele

Ke ne sachons, si le nus di,

E de quel terre tu viens ci.'   20

— 'Sire,' fait il, 'jo vieng de Rome

Ou jo laissai meint gentil home

Tuit corociez e trespensez,

Kar l'emperere est trespassez

De cest siecle novelement;   25

Si en tiennent grant parlement,

Kar il volent doner seignor

A la fille l'empereor,

Mes el refuse toz a orne

Kar sis pensers alliors li torne   30

En autre ou ele a son corage,

Pur qui jo ai fet cest grant vaage,

Mes ne trois pas ço que jo quier.'

— 'Messager, frere, or te requier

En servise e en geredon   35

Ke de celui me dites le non,

Aigres entre lui et son compaignon Orchas s'en alerent esbanoiant dehors le chastel de Dijon,

tant qu'il advint que ilz virent venir vers eulx grant alleure un messagier moult travaillié.

Et lors que cellui que Fortune menoit fut venue devant les barons, Aigres le salua premierement et aprez lui dist;

'Beaux doulx amiz, se Dieu te vueille aidier, se tu scez aucunes nouvelles, si les nous diz. Et si te requier par amours que tu nous dïes dont tu viens, s'il te plaist, et la ou tu vas.'

'Par ma foy,' dist le messagier, 'quant je meuz, je me parti de Romme, ou je laissay maint gentil chevalier et maint hault baron dollens et courrouciez pour l'empereur qui estoit nouvellement trespassez de cest siecle;

pour quoy ilz ont tenu et tiennent maint grant parlement, car ilz veullent donner mary a Milie la damoiselle de Romme, mais pour chose que ils lui sachent dire, admonnester ne prïer, elle n'en veult riens faire, car elle a donné son courage et son amour a un chevalier qui n'est mie ou païs, pour lequel j'ay ceste voie emprinse, mais je ne le puis trouver, dont il me poise durement pour vray.'

Quant Aigres oÿ nommer le nom de s'amie, si lui fremy toute la char, et dist lors au messagier: 'Frere, je te prie et requier en guerredon et en ser-

Ki tu si longement as quis;
Jo crei ja ne t'en serra pis.'

— 'Sires, Aigres,' fait il, 'a nom,
Si a od lui un compaignon   40
Ki Orchas estoit apellez.
Si ço estes vus, nel me celez,
Kar jo crei bien ço estes vus.'

— 'Amis, pur veir, ço sumes nos,'
Fait Aigres, 'bien es asenez.'   45
E li vallez, qui fu senez,
Si li baillie un seel de cire
Ke la pucele out fait escrire.
Il en a la cire brisee,
Si a la chartre desploiee,   50
E le parchemin desploia;
Mult sout bien tost quanqu'il i a.

vice que tu me dïes le nom de cellui que tu as si longuement quis.'

'Sire,' dist le message, 'sachiez qu'il a nom Aigres, et si a un compaignon avecques lui, qui Orchas est apellez. Pour Dieu, seigneurs, je vous pry que vous me disiez si c'estes vous, car le cuer me dist que vous estes ceulx que je quiers.'

'Certes,' dist Aigres, 'je te asseure que nous sommes ceulx que tu vas querant, et suis Aigres apellez, et mon compaignon que cy voiz, a nom Orchas.' Quant le messagier qui estoit sages et avisez, ot certainement enquis et entendu qu'il avoit trouvé ce que il queroit, si ot grant joie et puis bailla a Aigres unes lettres seellees de par la fille de l'empereur. Et tantost que Aigres les tint, il les ouvry et leut ce qu'il avoit dedens escript, si trouve en escript que s'amie lui mandoit salut comme celle qui avoit eü moult a souffrir pour lui.

Lines 3 and 4 are omitted, as being a conventional description of the season, which can be regarded as 'remplissage'; the reference to the horse (l. 7) is not thought to be of importance. Lines 9–11 are reproduced almost verbatim, but a slight change in line 9 destroys the rime correspondence. Line 14 is a platitude inserted for the sake of rime and is therefore omitted; as is line 16, for the messenger's news would explain whence he came. Slight changes of vocabulary and word-order destroy the rime and metre of lines 21–25. From line 26 to 33, the messenger's information is more detailed than it is in the verse; his anxiety is emphasised by an addition to line 33; probably the phrase 'a orne' (l. 29, 'in succession') would not have been understood by readers of the prose version. The speech of Aigres is introduced by a statement of his agitation; the verse equivalent begins abruptly, because the reciter would express by voice and gesture what the prose editor describes. For the same reason, the answer and the reply emphasise points which a reciter could have made verbally. The three lines which describe the opening of the letter are cut down to three words in the prose version.

Thus the *remanieur* kept pretty closely to the original. His changes were made to meet the taste of an audience belonging to a later generation than that for which the poem was composed, and to fulfil the requirements of a narrative intended for public or private reading, but not for dramatic recitation.

Such considerations naturally did not greatly concern translators of French works into their own language; they were not troubled with the task of obscuring rime or rhythm. An early Spanish translator of the *Roman de Troie* of Benoît de Sainte-Maure wrote in prose, but from time to time he intercalated his version with poetical renderings of passages or incidents which struck his imagination, in a manner that somewhat resembles the form of the French *chantefable*. Two brief extracts will sufficiently illustrate his methods; his prose keeps closely to the original; his verse is much more free.[1] Andromache has begged Hector not to join the battle.

Hector vers la dame s'iraist:
de quant qu'il ot rien ne li plaist;
ses paroles tient a falue,
irieement l'a respondue:
'des or', fait il, 'sai bien e vei,
n'en dot de rien ne nel mescrei,
qu'en vos n'a sen ne escïent.
trop avez pris grant hardement,
que tel chose m'avez nonciee,
se la folie avez songiee,
si la me venez reconter,
e chalongier e deveer
qu'armes ne port ne nc m'en isse;
mais ço n'iert ja, tant com jo puisse,
que jo les coilverz ne contende
e que jo d'eus ne me defende,
qui mon lignage m'ont ocis
e en ceste cité asis.
se li coilvert, li de put'aire,
öeïnt conter ne retraire,

E quando don Hector oyo aquesto, fue muy sañudo contra ella por aquello quel dexiera, e touolo por locura, e dixol: 'agora entiendo bien que non auedes seso ninguno e sodes muy atreuuida en me dezir tal cosa, e sy vos soñastes vuestra locura, ¿que cuydado he yo de auer por ende? E demas, que me fuestes defender que non presiese armas, lo que non puede ser, mientre yo sea biuo y sano; e syquier contra aquellos que son tan malos omes y tan soberuios e que mataron todo mi linaje e nos tienen aqui çercados.

E pues ¿commo puede ser que este yo aqui ençerrado e non salga a vengarme e a defenderme de aquellos? çertas, si lo sopiesen las gentes de la hueste e los

---

1 *Roman de Troie*, ll. 15,326 ff. The Spanish version has been edited by R. Menéndez Pidal, *Historia Troyana* en prosa y verso, texto de hacia 1270, Madrid, 1934 (*Revista de Filología Española*, Anejo xviii), p. 200.

e li chevalier d'este vile,
dont plus i a de dous cenz mile,
que d'un songe, se le songiez,
fusse si pris ne esmaiez
que je n'osasse fors eissir,
com me porroie plus honir?
ne vueille Deus que ço m'avienge
que por içq mort dot ne crienge!
n'en parlez mais, taisiez vos en,
quar n'en ferai ja vostre sen.'

de la villa, que son mas de dozientas
vezes mill caualleros, todos me ternian
por muy couarde e por muy malo, sy
yo, por espanto de los vuestros sueños,
dexase de tomar armas e de yr ayudar
a los mis hermanos; mas consejouos e
mandouos que de aqui adelante non
me enxequedes mas sobre esto, nin
vos lo entienda ninguno, ca fariades
a mi muy grand pesar e yo non lo
dexaria por ende.

Hector insists on going out to fight, in spite of Priam's prohibition, and Andromache's lamentation follows (*Roman*, l. 15,456; Spanish, p. 205):

Quant ele veit que el n'en iert,
o ses dous mains granz cous se fiert;
ses cheveus tuert e ront e tire,
fier duel demeine e fier martire:
bien resemble femme desvee.
tote enragiee, eschevelee
e trestote fors de son sen
cort por son fil Asternaten.
des ieuz plore mout tendrement,
entre ses braz le charge e prent;
vient el palais o tot arieres,
la ou chauçot ses genoillieres;
as piez se met e si li dit:
'sire, por cest enfant petit,
que tu engendras de ta char,
te pri, ne tienges a eschar

Andromaca, quando vio
la grand saña e grand brio
que Hector tomado auia
e la lid non dexaria,
de anbas sus manos ferie,
muy mal su rrostro rronpie,
de sus cabellos tiraua
e muy grand cuyta se daua
e muy grand duelo fazia
con grand rravia que avia;
e andaua commo loca
descabeñada, sin toca;
e fue con grande dolor
por su fijo el menor:
en los braços lo tomava
e al palaçio se tornaua,
grandes apellidos dando,
plañendo fuert e llorando.
Mas quando ella llegaua,
Ector a grand priesa estaua
las brafoneras calçando.
Ella muy cuytada, quando
vio que Ector asi yerra,
echose ante el en tierra;
dezie llorando: 'Ector,
mi amigo e mi señor,
¡ aved duelo d'este infante
que vedes aqui delante
que dexas tan pequeñuelo
pues de ti non aves duelo!

ço que jo t'ai dit e noncié;

aies de cest enfant pitié:

ja mais des ieuz ne te verra.

se assembles a ceus de la,

hui iert ta morz, hui iert ta fins:

de tei remandra orfelins.

crüeus de cuer, lous enragiez,

a que ne vos en prent pitiez?

por que volez si tost morir?

por que volez si tost guerpir

e mei e lui e vostre pere

e voz freres e vostre mere?

por que nos laissereiz perir?

com porrons nos senz vos guarir?

lasse, comfaite destinee!'

adonc chäi a denz pasmee

desus le pavement a quaz.

Por escarnio non lo tengas
lo que te digo, e non vengas
a muerte, e tu fijo biuo
venga a seer en catiuo
de griegos; e nos faremos.
Por tu culpa nos perdremos.

. . . .

¡ Lobo rravioso sin seso !
¿por que ora, por que ende,
algund duelo non te prende?
¡ Ay Ector !, ¿e que avedes
que asi morir queredes?
¿vos deuiades quexar,
ay mi señor, por dexar
a mi e a uuestro padre
e a hermanos e a madre.
a fijos e a parientes?
Por Dios, señor, meted mientes
en guardar la vuestra vida;
sinon, traes la perdida.
¡ Mi mesquina !, ¡ que ventura
mala, que fuerte, que dura !'
Andromaca esto dixie;
mas vio que non metie
Ector en tod esto mientes,
e dexo s'caer de dientes,
en tierra amorteçida
e fue maltrecha e ſerida
en el rrostro e en la cara;
tal commo muerta se para.

The Galician translation,[1] which belongs to the fourteenth century, does not appear to owe anything to the Spanish quoted above, and does not follow the French quite so closely. The passage given in Spanish prose is thus rendered by the Galician translator:

Eytor quando aquesto oyo pesoulle moyto, et asañousse moy ferament et touollo por gran loucura oquelle dissera, et rrespondeulle moy sañudo et dissolle assy. 'Agora sey eu ben et entendo que hun ponto de siso non auedes, et façome marauillado de uos seer tan ousada de prouar solament deme tal cousa dizer, et sse uos soñastes pouco syso non teño eu y que aduƀar nehuna cousa. Demays fostes dizer que non tomasse armas nen saysse da uila et esto non pode seer nen querran os dioses, que mentre eu uiuo for et poder tomar armas non

1 *Crónica Troyana*, por D. Manuel R. Rodriguez, La Coruña, 1900, I, p. 338.

peleie con aqueles soberuosos et auoles et maos que me mataron os parentes et os amigos et o liñagen todo, et nos aqui ueeron çercar, que me deles non defenda quanto poder. Et sse aqueles treedores et auoles esta rrazon oyssen et os outros que son ena uila, todos me terrian por uil et me preçiarian pouco. Et sse eu fosse desmaydo et leixasse de tomar armas e seyr da uila por uosso soño louco que soñastes, eu por ende ualrria menos, et non ha cousa por que eu mays cofondudo et mays auergonçado podesse seer, nen por que eu podesse buscar mayor meu daño. Ca ja deus nunca querria nen oteña por ben que eu por esto seia desmayado nen tema morte nen peligro. Et des agora uos castigo para senpre et uos defendo que nunca en tal pleito me faledes.'

The influence of narrative poetry upon prose will be obvious, if we go back to one of the first prose writers who was neither a poet nor a professional man of letters—Villehardouin. His chronicle of the crusade which started from Venice in 1202 was written between his retirement from active service and his death, between 1207 and 1213, and is the work of a plain soldier and administrator who avoids rhetoric and description, and is chiefly concerned to relate the facts as he saw and understood them. The chronicle was obviously written to be read aloud or recited; it may have been dictated to a scribe, though the statement that he 'ceste uevre dita' does not justify the inference; *diter* meant no more than 'compose', and has the sense of the curial Latin *dictare*, *dictamen*, *dictator*. But when we read 'plus doulereuse nouvele ne leur peüst on conter. La veïssiez mainte lerme plourer, et mainte paume batre de duel et de pitié', we suspect that the author of this sentence had some acquaintance with the *chansons de geste*. This impression is increased by the author's habit of using identical or nearly identical phrases to describe common actions of life whenever these occur; such formulae as 'chose la plus bele que on eüst onques veüe' are common. These features, with the impersonal and objective style, give an epic impression, due as much to the author's resolve to provide information as to any conscious or unconscious influence of the *chansons de geste*. Robert de Clari, a Picard noble, also took part in this fourth crusade and has left a narrative which contrasts strongly with the austerity of Villehardouin in its liveliness and descriptive power. Joinville, who took part in the sixth crusade some fifty years later, took notes of his experiences and his subsequent chronicle is characteristic of him—a writer who wanted to write, gifted with some power of observation but with little sense of proportion, who mistakes puerilities for facts of importance and babbles away in a style which is pleasant and agreeable, but has neither depth nor literary polish. These cases show that writers who had something to say, and were not obsessed by the necessity of translating or rehandling material provided by others, found that the prose language of their time was equal to their needs and were able to express their personality in their writing, in short, to develop what we now regard as an individual style.[1]

During the fifteenth century, prose was regarded as the obvious medium for the composition of works not only of erudition and instruction, but also of amusement. The Dukes of Burgundy maintained a succession of translators, compilers and adaptors of Latin works and of medieval tales and legends.[2] One of these was Jean Wauquelin, who worked for Philippe le Bon; of his productions there still remain a translation of the *Brut* of Geoffrey of Monmouth, a history of Alexander the Great which is a prose edition of the poem in alexandrine verse, attributed to several authors, a history of Girart de Roussillon, the *roman* of Helen of Constantinople, a translation of the *Gouvernement des Princes* by Gilles de Rome, and of the chronicle of the Dukes of Brabant, by Edmond de Dynter; Wauquelin also made a copy of Froissart, which has not come down to us. The Dukes demanded books in the grand style, fine folios, well written and magnificently illuminated, some of which are the most precious treasures of our modern libraries, and illuminators and binders were retained in the ducal service. Wauquelin's methods as an adaptor were not greatly different from those which have been already quoted. For his prose version of *Girart de Roussillon* he had apparently at his disposal the Latin life, the twelfth-century poem

1 Critics are not entirely agreed upon the extent to which the influence of epic style is perceptible in the work of Villehardouin. He told a plain tale and either avoided or did not know the devices of rhetoric. It has been argued that the turns of expression which remind us of the *chansons de geste* may equally well have come from popular speech, from which they certainly originated. The latest pronouncement is that of A. Jeanroy (*Histoire de la Nation française*, tome XII, Paris, 1921, p. 349): 'Il y a dans le style du maréchal de Champagne une sévérité, une gravité aristocratique d'où se dégage une impression de solennelle grandeur, accrue encore par ces formules épiques que notre prose naissante empruntait volontiers aux chansons de geste.'

2 See G. Doutrepont, *La Littérature française à la cour des Ducs de Bourgogne*, Paris, 1909; P. Meyer, *Girart de Roussillon*, Paris, 1884, pp. cxlii ff.; *Girart de Rossillon, poème bourguignon du XIVe siècle*, ed. E. B. Ham, Yale, 1939, p. 17. The works of Wauquelin fall between the dates 1445-53.

in a mixed French-Provençal dialect, and the fourteenth-century French *roman* in alexandrines, in Burgundian dialect. His prose version is a lengthy paraphrase of this last-mentioned poem; he makes attempts to conceal the extent of his debt to this poem, and occasionally refers to the other sources, but shows no particular anxiety to harmonise the discrepancies between them. Nor do his methods differ greatly from those of adaptors already mentioned. The opening lines of the thirteenth-century poem are:

> La chouse qui plus fait toute gent resjoÿr,
> C'est des diz et des faits des bons parler oÿr;
> Li bon bien les entendent et meilleur en deviennent,
> Ly malvais en amendent, maint autre bien en viennent.

Wauquelin attributes this saying to a 'sage', and paraphrases it thus:

Oïr dire, lire et recorder les beaulx dis et les bienfaiz des preudhommes est la chose au monde qui plus fait toutes bonnes gens resjouyr. Car les bons en deviennent meilleurs et les mauvais en amendent, et moult de biens en viennent.

Like most of his fellow adaptors, Wauquelin is dominated by the original, and is chiefly concerned to 'desrimer' it effectually. Style and individuality cannot be expected of prose produced under these conditions, and for such qualities we have to look elsewhere.

Did the Dukes read these magnificent folios? This, as has been said, is not a point upon which much information can be expected. M. Doutrepont (pp. 465 ff.) has collected some statements which affirm that Philippe le Bon read in the early morning when no other affairs occupied him; other nobles also either read for themselves or were read to, as a matter of habit. The libraries that many of them formed were not merely the outcome of collectors' mania; Jean d'Orléans, count of Angoulême, certainly read most of the 148 volumes which composed his library, as his marginal annotations show; the same seems to be true of René of Anjou. When nobility sets a fashion, it is usually followed by inferior social ranks, and the example of the Burgundian dukes no doubt encouraged a general interest in literature and reading. Naturally, the average household could not afford illuminated vellum folios; but during this century there is an increase in the number of those volumes composed of heterogeneous matter, in fact, miscellanies for family use. From these, someone could read aloud when amusement or instruction was desired during the winter evenings; at an earlier date Chrétien de Troyes describes, in *Yvain* (ll. 5362 ff.), a family party, where the daughter reads aloud to others who are illiterate:

> Yvain...
> Voit apoiié desor son cote
> Un riche home qui se gisoit
> Sor un drap de soie, et lisoit
> Une pucele devant lui
> An un romanz, ne sai de cui.
> Et por le romanz escouter
> S'i estoit venue acoter
> Une dame, et c'estoit sa mere
> Et li sires estoit ses pere,
> Si se pooient esjoir
> Mout de li veoir et oir.

To return from the twelfth century to the fourteenth, Froissart describes, in his *Dit du Florin*, how he read his interminable romance *Méliador*, more than 30,000 lines in length, to Gaston Phébus, the count of Foix. The romance is of interest, as giving a picture of aristocratic life in Froissart's time, but the intrigue is bewildering, the incidents are of stock character and the stage is overcrowded. However, the count seems to have enjoyed it. No one could improve Mme Darmesteter's description of the scene:

puis, vers le petit matin, on faisait la lecture à haute voix. Froissart s'étend sur les délices de ces séances. Il est vrai que c'était lui qui en était le héros. 'Tandis que je lisais, nous dit-il, personne ne devait parler ni mot dire, car le comte voulait que je fusse entendu.' La séance était intéressante au possible pour le lecteur, car c'était une œuvre de lui qu'il lisait au milieu de ce recueillement, un roman en vers qu'il avait apporté en cadeau au comte de Foix. Plaignons les malheureux courtisans condamnés pendant des semaines à écouter un interminable roman de la Table Ronde vers les trois heures du matin! Le comte, pourtant, ne ménageait pas son admiration:

> Il me dit: 'c'est un beau métier,
> Beau maître, de faire telles choses!'

Puis il tendait à l'auteur enroué, mais épanoui, la coupe où il venait de tremper ses lèvres. C'était la fin de la soirée. Les pauvres chevaliers, tombant de sommeil, rassemblaient leurs esprits à la hâte et se confondaient en éloges. Gaston

Phébus trouvait quelques mots aimables pour récompenser leur dévouement.... Enfin, il se levait, faisait une dernière fois circuler le vin et congédia sa cour exténuée.[1]

In England, during the second half of the fourteenth century, there was an increasing demand for literature of a secular nature written in English and not in French or Latin. Robert Mannyng of Brunne is best known for his *Handlyng Synne* composed in 1303 for the benefit of the uneducated, i.e. those who did not know French:

> For lewed men y undyrtoke
> On englyssh tunge to make thys boke.

About 1340 he produced a translation of Peter Langtoft's chronicle, his prologue to which has been several times quoted, in view of its bearing upon the position of English about this date. He says that he is writing for simple men who do not know 'strange English', and not for 'disours, seggers (reciters) or harpours'; hence for the benefit of the 'lewed men' he will avoid composing in 'ryme couwee or in strangere or enterlace' and will use a simple metre. He criticises other translators or adaptors, such as Thomas of Erceldoun, whose versions were not intelligible to the ordinary man:

> Thai sayd in so quante Inglis
> That manyone wate not what it is;
> Therfore I heuyed [hesitated] wele the more
> In strange ryme to trauayle sore;
> And my witte was ouer thynne
> So strange speche to trauayle in,
> And forsooth I couthe noght
> So strange Inglis as thai wroght,
> And menn besoght me many a tyme
> To turn it bot in lighte ryme.

So in the Prologue to *The Story of England* he says that he

> on Inglysch has it schewed
> not for the lerid bot for the lewed,
> ffor tho that in this lands wone
> that the Latyn no Frankys cone,

---

[1] *Les Grands Ecrivains français, Froissart,* Paris, 1891, p. 76; A. Scheler, *Œuvres de Froissart, Poésies,* Bruxelles, 1870, II, pp. 228–31.

> for to haf solace and gamen
> in felaweschip when thai sitt samen.

The story thus seems intended for reading aloud to a social gathering, as is also suggested by his use of repetitions for the benefit of late-comers or for inattentive hearers.[1]

There were thus three classes of readers; those who understood Latin or Anglo-Norman or both; those who preferred an elaborate and artificial diction of English, and those who required a plain tale simply told. It was for the last-mentioned that Robert proposed to provide. As he excluded professional minstrels or reciters, it must have been an ordinary reading public that he had in view.

Similar reasons may have produced the Romance of *William of Palerne*, a translation from the French, which was ordered by Sir Humphrey de Bohun, about 1350.[2] The translator concludes by calling upon his readers or hearers to pray for his patron:

> But, fair frendes, for goddes loue and for your owne mensk,[3]
> Ye that liken in loue swiche thinges to here,
> Preyes for that gode lord that gart this do make,
> The hende erl of hereford, humfray de boune;
> The gode king edwardes doughter was his dere moder;
> He let make this mater in this maner speche,
> For hem that knowe no frensche ne neuer understonde.

As the Earl was an important member of the court, he certainly would not have required a translation for his own use, for he must have known French. He probably wished to provide work for the translator and to benefit the same class for which Robert of Brunne made his versions.

A similar statement was made by John de Trevisa in the *Dialogue between a Lord and a Clerke*,[4] which was prefixed by Caxton to his edition of Higden's *Polychronicon*, printed in 1482; Trevisa's translation was made in 1387 at the instance of Thomas, Lord Berkely (Trevisa then held the living of Berkely in Gloucestershire). In the dialogue, the lord urges the making of English translations from Latin, for the benefit

---

1 See A. Kunz, *Robert Mannyng of Brunne's Handlyng Synne verglichen mit der anglonormannischen Vorlage, William of Wadington's Manuel des Pechiez*, Königsberg, 1913.
2 Ed. E.E.T.S. W. W. Skeat, 1867.
3 I.e. honour.
4 *John Wycliffe, also John de Trevisa*, by H. J. Wilkins, London, 1915, p. 94.

of the unlearned; the clerk objects to the translation of 'bokes that stondeth moche by holy Wrytte, by holy doctours and by philosophye', to which the lord replies that much work of the kind has been done, and gives as instances Alfred, Caedmon, Bede and others. The clerk's objections to the difficulty of translation are refuted, and he then puts the question, 'whether is you leuer haue a translacion of these Cronykes in Ryme or in prose?' The lord replies, 'in prose, for commonly prose is moore cleere than ryme, more easy and more playne to knowe and understande'. 'Thene', concludes the clerk, 'God grante us grace grathly to gynne, Witte and Wysedome wysely to worche, Myghte and mynde of right menynge to make translacion trusty and trewe, plesyng to the Trynyte thre persones and one God in mageste that euer was and euer shall be.'[1] The last sentence will serve to illustrate the difficulty with which the early prose writers abandoned the auditory impressions left by long acquaintance with verse. Not only Trevisa, but after him, John de Taystek, Richard Rolle of Hampole, William Nassyngton and others continually, and probably unconsciously, use synonymous word-pairs in alliteration and fall into the rhythmical structure of the four-stress line of alliterative verse. It may be that in their more emotional passages writers used these tricks for oratorical effect, as they were used in the thirteenth and sixteenth centuries. But it is difficult to avoid the impression that familiarity with verse coloured the first Middle English attempts to write prose. A further question was whether Latin words, for which no English equivalent existed, should be anglicised or paraphrased; opinion seems to have been averse to borrowing from Latin, and Wiclif's attempts to render Latin abstract terms in his native tongue often led to obscurity. His teaching upon the art of pulpit oratory was, in general, a direct attack upon the arts of the medieval rhetoricians; as Roger Bacon had argued before him from the humanistic point of view, so Wiclif denounced the use of oratorical ornament as likely to distract the attention of hearers from the matter under discussion. He demanded a plain, simple style, suited to the needs of simple folk, and he deserves the credit of having formulated the principles upon which a sound prose style should be based.

The famous Auchinleck manuscript, belonging to the Advocates Library of Edinburgh, has been more than once regarded as a miscellany which might well have been a family possession used for home reading

1 From the preface to the Caxton edition of 1482.

and entertainment. It was presented to the Library in 1744 by Alexander Boswell of Auchinleck, the father of James Boswell; of its earlier history nothing is known. It has suffered considerably from the mutilations of vandals; illuminations have been cut out and pages torn away. It now preserves 334 quarto pages of parchment, containing forty-four separate pieces; thirteen pieces have entirely disappeared. There remain eighteen romances, one chronicle and a list of Norman barons, two pious stories of the miracle type, eight legends of saints, the Purgatory of St Patrick, two debates between the Body and the Soul, the Thrush and the Nightingale, six pieces of a homiletic or religious character, three satirical pieces, and a humorous tale. Historical allusions show that the book was produced between 1330 and 1340; five scribes were employed upon it, and the dialect of two who did most of the work suggests that the book was produced in London, where, if anywhere, there was a reading public likely to be attracted by an English Miscellany of this kind. The romances make up the larger portion of the book, and this fact is in accordance with the complaint occasionally expressed, that people would read fiction in preference to religious truth.

It is generally admitted that the production of secular literature in English was, by the end of the fourteenth century, in the hands of translators and adaptors, of scribes and booksellers who were certainly non-clerical. 'Stationers' were certainly established in London during the first half of the fourteenth century, and the term *stationarius* implied dealing in books, as well as providing the material and the contents of them. It is possible that the Auchinleck manuscript was an early example of trade book production. The question has been examined and argued with much ingenuity by L. H. Loomis,[1] who concludes that the book was produced to order by some 'stationer' who had or could get a collection of texts for copying, and possibly employed hack translators or adaptors to produce versions of French originals; an examination of the texts shows that the authors and the copyists worked in some kind of association, the focal point of which was probably a London book shop. Such activity suggests the existence of a reading public more likely to be found in London than anywhere else in England, as in London were concentrated numbers of court and government officials who may be described as civil servants and who were likely to be

1 P.M.L.A. LVII (Sept. 1942), pp. 595 ff. This article contains useful references to literature bearing on the subject.

interested in English literature, while the citizens in general were better off and better educated than those of any other English town. The splendidly illuminated manuscripts produced in England during the fourteenth century were in French or Latin and were acquired by wealthy nobles and ecclesiastics; manuscripts in English were, as a rule, anything but *éditions de luxe*; they were intended for readers who could afford nothing elaborate.

Books, in the fourteenth and fifteenth centuries, were scarce and expensive, and were bequeathed in wills with other property of value. Some 7600 wills have been examined by M. Deanesly[1] and from her painstaking researches the following facts emerge. Only 338 books appeared as bequests in 7568 wills; before 1400 they were usually entailed, if left to an individual, or were bequeathed to the library of some community. It is thus obvious that few individuals possessed books; even priests owned no books except those of their office before 1400, and very few books after that date. Nor was access to libraries possible to any except a privileged few; such libraries belonged to cathedrals or collegiate churches and monastic orders, while small collections might be gathered by nobles, lawyers and university teachers. Vernacular books were scarce; Latin books were preponderant in number and French books were commoner than English before 1400; after that date English books increase in number, the majority being homiletic or devotional works and lives of the saints; few books are mentioned that might be classified as *belles-lettres*. Possibly these were not thought sufficiently valuable to form part of a bequest, or the practice of bequeathing 'my books' as a whole, which became more common after 1450, has concealed their titles. In any case, vernacular literature of the imaginative class was more likely to be read and borrowed than any other, and therefore more likely to disappear. To take a later case, few books are better known in Spanish literature than *Lazarillo de Tormes*; the earliest editions of this work were produced by three publishers in 1554; these were made independently from an earlier edition, perhaps of 1553. But this earlier edition has never been discovered. Probably no large number of copies were printed as a first edition and these were simply read to pieces.

To draw inferences from these or similar facts concerning the number of literate persons in any given population is hazardous; the proportion

1 *M.L.R.* xv (October 1920), p. 349.

naturally varied in different districts, provinces and countries, with the opportunities existing for education and with the prevailing degree of social culture. Francesco da Barberino (1264–1348), a lawyer who practised in Bologna and Florence and was well acquainted with Provençal literature, touched the question in his long-winded work *Del Reggimento e de' Costumi delle Donne*[1] in dealing with the education of women. Girls of high birth should learn to read and write, in view of their possible responsibilities in later years:

> E parmi, ch'a suo stato si convenga
> Che in questo tempo imprenda
> Leggere e scriver convenevolmente;
> Sicchè se convenisse
> Lei donna rimanere
> Di terra o di vassalli,
> Sarà più conta a reggimento fare.

For girls of lower birth, 'figliuola di Cavalier da Scudo, o di solenne Giudice, o di solenne Medico, o d'altro gentiluomo', Barberino doubts whether education is beneficial; having somewhat more freedom than the high-born, they are more likely to get into trouble:

> E questo è il tempo, nel quale a me pare,
> Che, se piace alli suoi,
> Imprender può leggere,
> Ed anco a scrivere alquanto con esto.
> Ma sovra questo punto
> Non so ben, ch'io mi dica:
> Che molti lodan ciò, e molti biasman ciò.

The conclusion, after arguments on either side, is:

> Ma in dubio pur pigliam la più sicura,
> E or m'accordo in questo,
> Ch'essa fatighi a imprendere altre cose,
> E quelle lasci stare.

Nuns and women in religious houses are exempted from these reservations, as they could not understand their service books, if they remained without education. An examination of the didactic treatises addressed

---

1 Rome, 1815, pp. 24 ff. See A. Thomas, *Francesco da Barberino et la littérature provençale en Italie au moyen âge*, Paris, 1883, p. 42.

to women[1] shows that Barberino's standpoint was generally adopted, when the question of education was considered. Reading and writing were upper-class accomplishments and were thought to be unnecessary for women whose household and family obligations were for them a full-time occupation. Daughters of merchants and common people, says Barberino, should

> Imprendere a fare
> Di molte più minute masserizie
> Che domandan le Case,
> Over conducimento delle Case.
> E meno in queste, che nell' altre dette,
> Lodo leggere o scrivere;
> Anzi lo biasmo.

In the *Libro de Apolonio*, composed in Spain about the middle of the thirteenth century, three suitors come forward for the hand of the king's daughter. The king asks them to send in written applications, stating their names and the amounts that they were prepared to settle on the lady (quatrain 209, b):

> Escreuit sendas cartas, ca escreuir sabedes;
> Escreuit vuestros nombres, que arras le daredes.

The king assumes that the young men, being princes, are certainly literate.

The Chronicle of James I of Aragon, of which the first part can hardly have been composed before 1230 (the first extant MS. is dated 1343), was apparently meant to be read aloud. Chap. I, ad fin. 'A aquells qui voldran ohir de las gracies que Nostre Senyor nos ha fetes, deixam aquest libre per memoria'. Chap. LXIX, ad fin. 'Per tal que sapigan aquells qui ohiran aquest libre que cara cosa fou d'armes co que fet fou en Mallorca'. But Chap. LXXII, ad init. 'Per tal que sapiguen aquells qui aquest libre veuran quantes partides hi ha en Mallorca'. The latter is a repetition of the formula used as preamble to legal documents; e.g. 'sapien tots homen qui aquesta Carta veuran com pau e treves foren tractades etc.'

As regarded England, Sir Thomas More, in his *Apologye* (1533),

---

1 A. A. Hentsch, *De la littérature didactique du moyen âge s'adressant spécialement aux femmes*, Cahors, 1903.

asserted that nearly half the population was illiterate. This estimate has been more than once attacked as an exaggeration; in any case, a distinction must be made between reading and writing, which were not acquired concurrently in the local schools, where writing was regarded as a superior skill. According to Leach, there were more schools in proportion to the population at the end of the fifteenth century than there were in 1864, if chantry schools, suppressed at the Reformation, and grammar schools are taken into account. Probably illiteracy was far more common in the country than in the towns, where the practice of posting bills on walls or distributing them indicates the existence of some reading public. References in the *Paston Letters* indicate that even among the servants of a household, some could be found able to keep accounts. In 1489 the rule concerning 'benefit of clergy' was changed; it was a privilege that laymen who could read had enjoyed with clergy from 1351. But during 150 years so many laymen had become literate that a distinction was drawn between them and ordained clergy.[1] On the whole, it may be said that any household of importance, in England, or abroad, contained at least one person who could read and write from the twelfth century onwards. He was often regarded with some amazement, and an explanation of the phenomenon was thought to be necessary. In the *Mort de Garin*, for instance,

> De letres sot li Loherens Garins,
> Car en s'enfance fu a escole mis
> Tant qu'il sot et Roman et Latin.

Aiol, ll. 273 ff.[2]

> Et Moisés l'ermite l'ot doctriné,
> De letres de gramaire l'ot escolé:
> Bien savoit Aiols lire et enbriever,
> Et latin et romans savoit parler.

Wolfram von Eschenbach, in the early thirteenth century, professed (at the end of *Parzival*, Book II) inability to read or write. If this were true, he must have had a prodigious memory and have gained his know-

---

1 *The Paston Letters*, ed. J. Gairdner, London, 1875, III, p. lvii. J. W. Adamson, *The Extent of Literacy in England in the Fifteenth and Sixteenth Centuries*, in *The Library*, x, no. 2 (September 1929), p. 163, is a valuable and learned article on this point.

2 A.T.F. ed. Normand et Raynaud, 1877. Date, 1205–1215.

ledge of the French originals of his work by hearing them read or having them translated to him. Possibly his declaration was a pose, adopted to distinguish his position from that of the ordinary scribe or composer. His contemporary, Ulrich von Lichtenstein, the author of *Frauendienst*, said that he relied upon a secretary to read his lady's letters to him. In every country, men of high rank usually employed a secretary to write their letters for them, but generally after the fourteenth century signed them in autograph, often in a fearful scrawl which taxes the competence of the palaeographer, and it is hardly to be thought that they would sign what they could not read. But, as has been said elsewhere, the subject is one that concerns those daily habits which contemporary writers take for granted and hardly mention; hence we are reduced to such inference as can be made from scattered and scanty evidence.[1]

The development of a vernacular prose is thus the resultant of two converging influences; a state or province which is able to dominate its neighbours will eventually impose its language upon them, the more readily if they speak a dialect akin to that of the dominant power; the necessity for an official language in which administration can be conducted will inevitably lead to the use of a common vernacular. Such a vernacular will already have been placed upon a literary basis by the work of poets and reciters; when private individuals begin to read for

1 Mr Adamson quotes the case of the contemporary continuator of Knighton's *Chronicon* under date 1381–82, who complains that Wiclif's translation of the Gospel...vulgarised the text and made it more accessible to layfolk 'legere scientibus' than to 'clericis admodum literatis', and adds the fact that vernacular or glossed versions of the *Primer* began to appear about the same time. Prohibitions of the use of vernacular copies of the Scriptures appear sporadically in all countries at a much earlier date. It seems dangerous to use such proclamations as evidence of any widespread literacy in a population. One reader is quite able to spread 'heresy' among an illiterate population, if he can get others to listen to him. The attitude of the medieval church to the question of translations was somewhat inconsistent; the principle of translation was not contested, and could not be, in view of the fact that Latin Christianity was founded upon the work of Jerome—the Vulgate. So translations of the Scriptures were made for royal personages or members of the upper classes, often in magnificent form, and to these no objections were raised; but if an attempt was made to spread knowledge of the biblical text among the laity, prohibition at once followed. See M. Deanesly, *The Lollard Bible*, Cambridge, 1920, who discusses the whole question with a wealth of examples and concludes that the attitude of the church was 'toleration in principle and distrust in practice'.

themselves and the demand for information as well as for amusement creates an appreciation of prose, the final stage of development has been reached. Such was the case in France and in Spain, where Francien and Castilian became official languages and therefore literary languages, which poetry had already created and popularised. In England, if Anglo-Norman seemed at one time likely to overpower Anglo-Saxon, so soon as the Angevin empire declined and continental connections were weakened, Middle English advanced rapidly. In Italy, conditions were very different. There was no one state capable of gaining and maintaining political supremacy in the peninsula, and none that seemed likely to do so, after the decline of the Hohenstaufens in Sicily; men of learning were also inclined to hold the vulgar tongue in contempt and to write in Latin, or in French and Provençal, if they wished to use a vernacular. Of Dante's conviction that an Italian vernacular could be formed, which could become national, we have already spoken with reference to his ideas upon style. Unfortunately, his treatise, *De Vulgari Eloquentia*, remained unfinished, and the part of it which we do not possess contained, or would have contained, his theories upon prose style.

For some indication of these, we have to go to his *Convivio*. This work was composed between 1304 and 1307, while the *De Vulgari Eloquentia* probably belonged to 1303–4. It is likely that he had both treatises upon the stocks at the same time, and that his reference in the *Convivio* (I, v, 10) to a 'libello ch'io intendo di fare' refers to the completion and publication of the *De Vulgari Eloquentia* rather than to the writing of it as a whole. The *De Vulgari Eloquentia* was written in Latin, because Dante wished to appeal to the scholars who despised books in the vernacular, and to convert them to his views. The *Convivio* was to show scholars of what the vernacular was capable; in it could be conducted discussions upon points of scholastic philosophy for which hitherto Latin had been regarded as indispensable. This *vulgare illustre* is also called *aulicum* and *curiale*, as being a language fitted for use by courts and governments and so contributing to the formation of the national unity which Dante regarded as the great ideal and for which he argued in the *De Monarchia*.

In this case, again, prose is made possible by the work of the poets. The writers of the *stil nuovo* had shown the possibility of amalgamating dialectical elements from different parts of Italy with a basic flux of

Florentine; this fact, with Dante's knowledge of the Provençal κοινή, doubtless started him upon his course of investigation. Dante's prose, as seen in the *Convivio*, suggests that his theory followed the principles already laid down for poetry in the *De Vulgari Eloquentia*. When he says, in the *Convivio* (I, iv, 13), that he is using a *più alto stilo* than that of the *Vita Nuova*, in order to 'impart to the present work something of gravity, by which it may seem of greater authority', he implies that the theory of the three styles, expounded in the *De Vulgari Eloquentia*, is applicable also to prose. In the prologue to the *Convivio* he follows the rules of the *cursus* and no doubt had in mind the rules for composing epistolary prose, as adopted by the Roman curia; these rules were codified in handbooks known as *summa dictaminis*, and the terms *dictamen* and *dictatores*, by which composition and writer under the system were known, are used by Dante in the *De Vulgari Eloquentia*.[1]

1 See *M.L.R.* XXXVII (1942), pp. 156 ff.: *Links between the 'Convivio' and the 'De Vulgari Eloquentia'*, by R. Weiss.

CHAPTER VI

PUBLICATION & CIRCULATION

BEFORE the invention of printing, the work of publication was performed by a special class of travelling or wandering artists, who were, in the South of France, differentiated from the poets; the performer was the *joglar*, the composer, the *trobador*.[1] The line of demarcation between the two was not very definite; the joglar might rise to the troubadour class, if he were a man of ability; the troubadour might fall upon evil days and earn his living by performance of other men's works. Normally, the troubadour was attached to the court of some noble or settled upon his own domain, whence he sent out his joglars to present his compositions either to a particular person, or to a court or a district. The two, between them, provided amusement for the aristocratic feudal society of their time. In Northern France, the *jongleur* bore a name of wider meaning; he might be a composer as well as a performer, and his performance might present not merely poetry, but circus and juggling tricks, performing animals, or anything that would amuse the audience before him. Jongleurs who were definitely attached to a household or court might be known as *ménestrels*.

A poet's reputation was thus dependent to a large extent upon the ability of his jongleur, who was expected to learn and to perform a composition while accompanying himself upon an instrument, in the case of lyric poetry, the tune being quite as important a matter as the words. Hence poems sometimes conclude with a 'tornada' or envoi, urging the jongleur to do his best, or expressing fear that a bad performer may spoil the work; poems survive in which troubadours criticise in no measured terms the talents and performance of the jongleur, who was expected to perform from memory and to have a considerable repertoire at his command. Jaufre Rudel, prince of Blaye, sends

1 On this subject, the most complete study is that of E. Faral, *Les Jongleurs en France au Moyen Age*, Paris, 1910.

a poem by his joglar, Filhol, who is not provided with a written copy:

> Senes breu de parguamina
> Tramet lo vers en chantan
> En plana lengua romana
> A.n Ugo Brun, per Filhol.

Petrarch describes them as 'Homines non magni ingenii, magnae vero memoriae, magnaeque diligentiae' with other less favourable observations.[1] Giraut de Cabreira blamed his joglar Cabra for incompetence in singing and instrumental accompaniment, for inability to perform tricks or to dance, and for ignorance of a formidable list of epic poems which no human being could be expected to master in their entirety. This satire suggests that the professional entertainer usually possessed an extensive repertoire which included the recitation of epic as well as the performance of lyric poems.[2] The feats of memory involved were probably less surprising to a medieval audience than they would be to ourselves. Our memories have been impaired by print; we know that we need not 'burden our memories' with matter which we can find merely by taking a book from a shelf. When a large proportion of a population is illiterate and books are scarce, memories are often tenacious to a degree outside modern European experience. Indian students are able to learn a text-book by heart and to reproduce it word for word in an examination room; sacred texts are preserved intact by oral transmission alone. 'It is said that if all the written and printed copies of the Rigveda were lost, the text could be restored at once with complete accuracy.'[3] This text is about as long as the *Iliad* and *Odyssey* combined. Russian and Jugoslav oral poetry is recited by minstrels who show great powers both of memory and of improvisation.

The Waldensians were constantly charged by inquisitors with knowing large portions of the Scriptures by heart. Etienne de Bourbon, writing about 1246, says: 'Vidi ego juvenem bubulcum, qui solum per annum moram fecerat in domo cujusdam heretici Valdensis, qui tam diligenti attencione et sollicita ruminacione affirmabat et retinebat que

1 Faral, pp. 75, 76.

2 Cp. the claims to omniscience put forth by Peire de Corbian in his *Tesaur*, ed. Jeanroy, *Ann. du Midi*, year 1911, p. 289.

3 Chadwick, *The Growth of Literature*, Cambridge, 1936, II, pp. 437, 463.

audiebat, quod infra annum illum firmaverat et retinuerat quadraginta evangelia dominicalia, exceptis festivitatibus, que omnia verbo ad verbum in lingua sua didicerat, exceptis aliis verbis sermonum et oracionum. Vidi eciam aliquos laicos qui ita erant eorum doctrina imbuti, ut vel multa de evangelistis, ut Mattheum vel Lucam, repeterent infra corde, maxime ea que ibi dicuntur de instructione et sermonibus Domini, ut vix ibi in verbis deficerent quin ea successive continuarent.' Others were said to have known by heart the whole of the New Testament and parts of the Old Testament.[1]

No less impressive is the case of Iceland, where masses of verse have been preserved by no other means than that of oral tradition. Sir William Craigie quotes a pertinent case.[2] 'Another set of *rimur* composed by the same author (Sigurður Bjarnason) in 1862 has had a remarkable history. No manuscript of these has been preserved, but a younger brother learned them by heart at the age of fifteen, and at the same time noted the first line of each verse. Fifty-five years later, in Canada, and without having gone over them in his mind for thirty years, he dictated the whole of them, to the extent of 4000 lines, and they were printed at Winnipeg in 1919. This is not only significant for the history of Icelandic poetry but for that of some other literatures, where the possibility of such feats of memory has been gravely questioned by scholars of the present day.'

The professional reciter undoubtedly sought to enliven his performance by the use of gesture and changes of voice when, for instance, he impersonated the interlocutors in a dialogue. When he recited,

> Dist Blancandrins: 'Par ceste meie destre,
> E par la barbe ki a.l piz me ventelet...

(*Roland*, l. 47), he could raise his right hand clenched and sweep his left across his breast. This could not be done by a performer holding a manuscript in one hand and refreshing his memory by glances at it. The jongleur had to know his stuff absolutely by heart, and his repertoire had to include many more poems than one. This dramatic mode of recitation will explain certain features in early French syntax, such

---

1 *Anecdotes Historiques d'Etienne de Bourbon*, par A. Lecoy de la Marche, Paris, 1877, p. 309; M. Deanesly, *The Lollard Bible*, Cambridge, 1920, p. 62. See also Radolphus de Coggeshale, Rolls Series, p. 123, on the Publicani heretics.

2 *The Art of Poetry in Iceland*, Taylorian Lecture, 1937, p. 32.

as the constant use of asyndeton and the change of tense in descriptive passages.[1] It is thus likely that competent jongleurs possessed wide and retentive memories, and here may lie the solution of a point that has troubled historians of literature; the case is stated by Bédier as follows:[2] 'Certaines chansons de geste, et des plus célèbres, nous sont parvenues en deux, trois, voire quatre rédactions, qui, sensiblement contemporaines les unes des autres, font double, triple, quadruple emploi. Comment est-ce possible? Que, vers l'an 1170, un versificateur ait voulu rajeunir, en vue de mieux plaire, la *Chanson de Roland*, celle que nous offre le manuscrit d'Oxford, remplacer les assonances par des rimes exactes, retrancher certaines scènes, développer certaines autres, délayer par exemple l'épisode de Bele Aude, rien de plus naturel; nous pouvons déplorer son mauvais goût, nous comprenons du moins ses intentions. Ce qui est plus surprenant, c'est que son rajeunissement nous soit parvenu sous deux formes: la leçon des manuscrits de Châteauroux et de Venise d'une part, la leçon des manuscrits de Paris, de Cambridge et de Lyon d'autre part. Ce sont deux rédactions qui offrent chacune certains épisodes ou traits particuliers, mais qui à l'ordinaire se suivent strophe pour strophe, presque phrase pour phrase, et pourtant de telle sorte que, dans ces strophes qui racontent la même scène, dans ces phrases qui expriment la même pensée, il y ait rarement deux vers identiques. Ainsi pendant dix ou douze milliers de vers. Or, la philologie parviendra peut-être un jour à déterminer que la version Châteauroux-Venise est la plus ancienne des deux ou inversement; mais jamais la critique littéraire ne pourra expliquer, par des motifs littéraires, qu'un homme ait eu la fantaisie, ou plutôt l'absurde courage, de rimer la version Châteauroux-Venise, puisqu'il connaissait l'autre, ou inversement. Qu'est-ce, si l'on considère que les dix-huit mille vers de *Renaud de Montauban* ont été récrits selon le même système; et pareillement le *Couronnement de Louis*, le *Charroi de Nîmes*, la *Prise d'Orange*, les *Enfances Vivien*, la *Chevalerie Vivien*, etc., une très longue série de chansons du cycle de Garin de Monglane, qui nous sont parvenues en trois ou en quatre rédactions à peu près contemporaines, continûment dissemblables,

1 See Appendix A, and *On the Use of Tenses in Old and Middle French*, by D. R. Sutherland, in *Studies Presented to M. K. Pope*, Manchester University Press, 1939, p. 329.

2 *Histoire de la Nation française*, tome XII (*Histoire des Lettres*, vol. 1), Paris, 1921, p. 232.

continûment identiques. C'est une série de faits sans analogue dans l'histoire d'une littérature quelconque.'

But a series of analogous facts can be found. The Jugoslav minstrel 'depends more upon improvisation[1] than memory. He need hear a poem only two or three times in order to reproduce it; but the reproduction is by no means given in the same words. To a certain extent every minstrel is a more or less creative poet. But a poem is never repeated in exactly the same words even by the same man; and in the course of years changes may be introduced which apparently render it almost unrecognisable. Cases are known of minstrels who have doubled and even trebled the length of poems which they had heard.'[2] So a jongleur who heard a poem recited which pleased the public and brought gain to the artist, might well desire to add it to his repertoire. The said performer would naturally wish to retain the monopoly; but a jongleur who knew his business would have no trouble in recalling the succession of incidents and even much of the language after two or three hearings; his profession had provided him with a large store of rimes, commonplaces and other padding, and if his first recitation proved successful he would elaborate the version and eventually reduce it to writing. The history of ideas upon literary copyright remains to be written; but even in days before print, cases occur of authors who were anxious to secure a monopoly of their own productions. Lyric poets complicated their rime schemes to prevent interpolations by the unscrupulous; Dante's terza rima is a case in point; even so, stanzas and 'tornadas' were

1 The Triumph of St Rémacle is a case of improvisation. 'Cantor quidam jocularis ipsa nocte cum sodali suo apud hospitium dormitum ierat, qui statim somno excitatus:

> Sodes, ait, surge; nos illo praestat abire:
> Non est hoc vanum; non est hic, crede, morandum;
> Excubias illas celebrare juvat venerandas.

Cumque ille renuens eum erroneae visionis argueret: Non fallor, ait, somno ludificante; sed testor Deum, quemdam venerandi habitus, quasi manu apprehensa, me illuc trahentem vidisse. Quibus dictis, praepeti cursu se contulit inter vigiles, ac ignarus quid caneret, fortuitu

> Coepit de Sancto percurrere plura canendo,

ac nostros digestim referendo casus, tristes sua quodammodo solabatur cantilena, choreis concinentibus.' (End of eleventh century; *Leodiensium historia*, tome II, p. 561, Du Méril, *Mélanges archéologiques*, p. 300.)

2 See Chadwick, *loc. cit.*

occasionally added by jongleurs for their own purposes. Troubadour rime schemes and tunes were regarded as the property of the composer and anyone who borrowed them was expected to make acknowledgement. The same convention existed in Germany until the middle of the thirteenth century, when plagiarism became common. To preserve the monopoly of an epic poem was more difficult. The following instances are instructive.[1] The prologue to the *Bataille Loquifer*:

> Ceste cançons est faite grant pieça.
> Por voir vous di .C. et .L. ans a
> Grandors de Brie, qui les vers en trova,
> Por sa bonte si tres bien le garda,
> C'ains a nul home ne l'aprist n'ensigna.
> Maint grant avoir en ot et conquesta
> Entor Sesile u li bers conviersa.
> Quant il fu mors a son fil le douna.
> Li rois Guillaumes tant celui losenga,
> Que la cançon de devers lui saça,
> Ens en .I. livre le mist et saiela.
> Quant il le sot, grand dolor en mena:
> Puis ne fu sains tant come il dura.

Graindor is unknown; the statement is that he composed the poem a century and a half before the prologue was written (in itself, a somewhat suspicious assertion), that the poem was so successful and brought in so much profit that he kept it to himself. When he bequeathed it to his son, King William persuaded the son to hand it over, and produced it in manuscript, to the great annoyance of the owner. In the prologue to *Doon de Nanteuil* the jongleur says that he will relate a very popular tale:

> Je vous en dirai d'une qui molt est henoree:
> El riaume de France n'a nule si loee.
> Huon de Villenoeve l'a molt estroit gardee;
> N'en volt prendre cheval ne la mule afeltree,
> Peliçon vair ne gris, mantel, chape forree,
> Ne de buens paresis une grant henepee.
> Or en ait il maus grez, qu'ele li est emblee!
> Une molt riche piece vos en ai aportee.

1 Faral, pp. 179, 182, 195.

The jongleur says that Huon de Villeneuve had a poem which was so successful that he would not part with his rights for any number of presents; the poem was stolen from him, much to his disgust, and the jongleur is now able to recite a 'rich part' of it. He does not profess to recite the original, and his version may have been one put together by some jongleur who had been present at recitations by Huon. The prologue to *Les Enfances Guillaume* gives the following account of its composition:

> Uns gentis moines qui a Saint Denis iert,
> Quant il oït de Guillaume parleir,
> Avis li fut que fust entrobliés.
> Si nos en ait les vers renovellés
> Qui ont el role plus de cent ans esteis.
> Je li ai tant et promis et donnés,
> Si m'a les vers enseigniés et monstrés.

In this case the monk who had brought the epic to light did not apparently wish to make use of it himself, but some persuasion was needed before he would release it for publication.

It is possible, as Faral suggests, that these accounts of literary origins were invented to impress the audience with the antiquity and interest of the poems to be recited, as Cervantes referred to the *Historia de Don Quijote de la Mancha, escrita por Cide Hamete Benengeli, historiador arábigo* (a form of mystification that has been used by authors in every age), perhaps in parody of the title which Perez de Hita prefixed to his *Guerras Civiles de Granada*. But such fictions would be pointless, if they did not appeal to the sentiments of the age, they show that authors not only attempted to secure a monopoly of a good narrative, but to protect it from the piracy of other jongleurs by asserting that the only authoritative version was in their possession and that other versions were the work of incompetent bunglers. Thus the author of *Les Enfances Ogier* (ed. Scheler, l. 13) declares

> Cil jougleor qui ne sorent rimer,
> Ne firent force fors que dou tans passer;
> L'estoire firent en pluseurs lieus fausser.

So in *Gaufrey* (Faral, *op. cit.* p. 192):

> Poi trouverés jouglierre qui de chesti vous chant;
> Quar il en est moult poi qui sache le romand.

The author of *Florence de Rome* (ed. A. Wallerskold, A.T.F. 1907)
insists more than once that the interest of his narrative is due to its
historical veracity:

> Seignor, iceste estoire n'est pas d'ui ni d'ier,
> Ains est vielle et antive du tens anciennier. (l. 1255.)
> . . . .
>
> Nostre chanson commence imes a esforsier;
> Juglaor que la chante ne fet a mesprisier,
> Ains le doit l'en forment loer et essaucier.
> La chanson est d'estoire, ce vos vuel acointier;
> Ainz ne fu tel trovee des le tens Dessier.

'Our song now begins to increase in interest; a jongleur who sings it is not
to be despised; on the contrary, he should be highly praised and complimented.
I would have you know that the song is historical; none such has been composed
since the time of Didier' (a legendary Lombard king, l. 5245).

Joufrois, 2324:

> Escouter moi, si orrez sa vie
> Ensi, cum ele me fu dite
> La, u ge la trovai escrite
> A saint Peire de Maguelone.
> Des lo main i mis jusqu'a none,
> Ainz que j'en fusse a la fin.
> Iluec la getai de Latin;
> Despuis si l'ai en rime misse
> Et en romanz l'estoire asisse.

Orson de Beauvais, A.T.F. 1899 (date, 1180–1185), ll. 2527 ff.:

> Des ici en avant orrez bone chançon,
> Tote la verite, outre n'en set nus on,
> Si come il est escrit, et cil de Beauvais l'ont,
> Au grant mostier Saint Pierre, ou li chanoine ṣont:
> Iluec porrez trover le vieil rolle d'Orson,
> Ensi con li escriz fu seelez en plon:
> Si la vos redirons que ja n'en mentirons,
> Tote la grant estoire de la grant traïson.

The Provençal version of *Fierabras* (l. 5) makes a similar claim:

> L'estoria fon trobada a Paris sotz l'autar,
> que la trobet us monge c'om apela Richier,
> al mostier Sant Denis sotz lo maestre-autier.

Saint-Denis had a great reputation as a monastery in which historical records were preserved. For references to other monasteries, see Gautier, *L'Epopée française*, I, p. 118; III, pp. 242 ff. The pretended discovery of a manuscript under such conditions was intended to inspire the audience with a belief in the authenticity of the narrative and to assure them that they were to hear something new, and something which they could not hear from any other source, except from the jongleur who had a monopoly of the story.

None the less, it was difficult for a jongleur to protect himself from the piracy of rivals, who might be capable of producing independent versions of his theme, if they were able to hear recitations of it. To give a public recitation of a poem was to make it common property. The ideas that we associate with such terms as 'plagiarism', 'copyright', or 'author's rights' simply did not exist and were not likely to exist until the invention of printing had revolutionised methods of publication. As has been said, troubadours were expected to acknowledge the borrowing of a rime-scheme or of a tune, but this seems to have been a convention based upon public opinion; a poet with a reputation to lose would not care to have it said that he lived upon the works of other authors. In Spain Juan I of Aragon in 1377 allowed his court minstrels to visit Castile for the wedding of the son of the Marquis of Villena and to teach their new songs to the minstrels of the Marquis.[1] But control of this kind was exceptional. No one troubled about an author, as long as he did not publish heresy or slander, and no one had any compunction in borrowing what they pleased from his works. For instance, the author of the *Roman de la Violette* (composed about 1275; ed. A.T.F. 1928) borrowed liberally from the *Comte de Poitiers* and from the *Roman de la Rose*. He knew the works of Chrétien de Troyes and took two episodes from *Yvain*, and also one from *Perceval* and one from *Erec*. *Tristan*, *Florence de Rome*, *Fierabras*, *Meraugis de Portlesguez* were also occasional sources of his inspiration.[2]

Jehan Makaraume, a Walloon, who wrote about the middle of the thirteenth century, produced a verse translation of the Bible, into which he introduced the *Roman de Troie* of Benoît de Sainte-Maure with some

1 Menéndez Pidal, *Poesía Juglaresca*, p. 446 and references there given.
2 For other cases in detail, see M. Wilmotte, *Le Poème de Galeran*, in *Bull. Acad. Royale de Belgique*, 5 sér., tome XIV (1928), nos. 7–9, pp. 269–309; G. L. Hamilton, *Mélanges offerts à M. Alfred Jeanroy*, Paris, 1928, *Encore un Plagiat*, p. 627.

abbreviation and modification. In the words of the editor of the *Roman de Troie* (L. Constans, A.T.F. vol. VI, p. 39): 'moins scrupuleux encore que la plupart des écrivains du moyen-âge, qui cependant ne l'étaient guère, Makaraume ne s'est pas contenté d'emprunter à un versificateur de talent, qui avait signé jusqu'à quatre fois son œuvre, un poème qu'il jugeait devoir plaire à ses lecteurs: il se l'est approprié en le démarquant de la façon suivante. Au Prologue, vers 131–4 (au lieu de: Ja retraite ne fust ancore, Mais Beneeiz de Sainte More L'a controve e fait e dit E o sa main les moz escrit) il dit: Ne ancor ne fust elle traite, Ne fust Jehans qui l'a refaite, Makaraumes dis a sornon, L'a remise en tel sermon Et comencie et faite et dite Et a ses mains l'a tote escrite.' The other three passages are similarly rewritten, or rather botched, in support of the claim of Makaraume to the authorship of the poem.

Prose writers and chroniclers followed this example. 'Bernard le Trésorier a vécu et s'est fait un nom de l'œuvre d'autrui. Il ne mettait du reste à son travail ni ruse ni malice, et ne comptait pas en tirer vanité. Comme tant d'autres chroniqueurs, il est le plus naïf plagiaire. Il copie presque mot pour mot la chronique de son prédécesseur en conservant les formes les plus personnelles de la rédaction....Les écrivains du moyen-âge, chez qui la modestie excuse le plagiat, supprimaient souvent le nom des écrivains dont ils reproduisaient le travail; eux-mêmes négligent fréquemment de se nommer, de sorte que leurs rédactions diverses rattachées à celles qui les précèdent et qui les suivent par quelques phrases du dernier continuateur ou des compilateurs, paraissent former au premier abord une œuvre unique et homogène. L'appropriation des chroniques antérieures va quelquefois plus loin. Divers écrivains, Jean d'Ypres, par exemple...semblent raconter comme témoins oculaires des événements dont ils sont éloignés de plusieurs siècles.'[1] The lack of public sentiment upon the question of authorship is shown by the fact that the *chansons de geste* are usually anonymous, at any rate in the manuscripts that have come down to us; some of the *remanieurs* attempt to claim authorship by the use of anagram or acrostic concealing their names. The prose romances of which the authors are known are outnumbered by the anonymous; professional translators, such as David Aubert or Jean Wauquelin, naturally advertised their profession by announcing their names in prefaces or elsewhere.

1 *Chronique d'Ernoul et de Bernard le Trésorier*, par M. L. de Mas Latrie, Paris, 1871, p. xxix and p. 489.

On the basis of these considerations can be explained the co-existence of similar versions of a poem, the resemblance between which obliges the critic to assume their descent from a single source, but the difference between which makes the establishment of a line of filiation impossible. Bédier proposed to explain the co-existence of these versions as the product of confraternities of jongleurs in rivalry with one another, on the ground that the task of writing out the sixty or eighty thousand verses which make up such a cycle as that of Monglane would be too much for any one man to undertake. The hypothesis seems to raise more difficulties than it solves. There is no cogent evidence to suggest that confraternities of jongleurs devoted themselves to the mass production of epics; there is much evidence to show that the individual jongleur worked for his own benefit and that, like Molière, he 'prenaits on bien partout où il le trouvait'.

Sir Beves of Hamtoun, to give it its English name, is a story which spread into most of the European literary vernaculars. Two versions, nearly contemporary, exist in the body of literature known as Franco-Italian; in the words of Pio Rajna, 'il gergo del testo laurenziano è dialetto veneto, mentre nel marciano troviamo una stranissima mistura in cui prevale la lingua d'oïl. Ma certo nè l'uno nè l'altro linguaggio furono mai parlati quali noi li troviamo in questi documenti; v'ha sempre qui dentro qualcosa di artefatto, parole, frasi ed anche inflessioni di origine forestiera.' To this characteristic, reference has been already made. From a comparison of the two texts, Rajna concluded 'che la narrazione dovette trasmettersi di bocca in bocca...nessuno dei due testi si può tenere trascrizione di quello che trasportò premieramente in Italia la storia di Buovo, sibbene entrambi furono composti dietro reminiscenze, sicchè ora l'uno ora l'altro riuscì più fedele. Con questa ipotesi s'accorda assai bene il fatto che di tempo in tempo qualche verso, qualche parola nei due testi si accorda, mentre poi solitamente la forma differisce al tutto, togliendo così ogni ragione di sospettare che l'uno dei due autori scrivesse tenendo sotto gli occhi l'opera dell'altro. Quale delle due versioni sia stata composta la prima, non saprei dire: ambedue credo s'abbiano a collocare tra il 1250 e il 1330.'[1]

1 *Ricerche intorno ai Reali di Francia*, per Pio Rajna, Bologna, 1872, I, p. 144. As an example of the 'stranissima mistura' the following may serve:
'El vete una nave chi vol passar lo mar.
Li mercadanti voleva a nave andar;

Composition upon a memory basis is a possible explanation of certain characteristics apparent in the early *Chanson de Sainte Foy* (ed. E. Hoepffner and P. Alfaric, *Publications de la Faculté des Lettres de l'Université de Strasbourg*, Paris, 1926). The opening *laisses* insist upon the fact that the poet gained his material by listening to a recitation of the Latin version or versions of the legend:

> Legir audi sotz eiss un pin
> Del vell temps un libre latin;
> Tot l'escoltei tro a la fin:
> Hanc non fo senz, q'el non.l declin.
> 5 Parled del paire al rei Licin
> E del linnadg' a Maximin.
>
> . . . .
>
> Canczon audi q'es bella 'n tresca,
> 15 Que fo de razon espanesca;
> Non fo de paraulla grezesca
> Ne de lengua serrazinesca.
>
> . . . .
>
> 20 Qi ben la diz a lei francesca,
> Cuig me qe sos granz pros l'en cresca
> E q'en est segle l'en paresca
>
> . . . .
>
> Eu l'audi legir a clerczons
> Et a gramadis, a molt bons,
> Si qon o monstra.l passions
> 30 En que om lig estas leiczons.
> E si vos plaz est nostre sons,
> Aisi con.l guida.l primers tons,
> Eu la vos cantarei en dons.

'I heard read aloud under a pine-tree a Latin book of old time; I listened to it right to the end; there was no meaning which it did not make clear. It spoke

---

> La barcha era a terra per doverli portar.
> Bovo ali mercadanti prexe a parlar.
> "Signor", disse Bovo, "or m'ascoltà.
> Eo son cristian e sì son batiçà;
> De la prixon del Soldan son scanpà;
> Un ano e tre mexi son demorà.
> Eo ve prego per Dio che me façè portar;
> In santa tristentade voio andar."'

of the father of King Licinus and of the lineage of Maximinus....I heard a song which is fair in dancing, which was on a Spanish subject; it was not of Greek tongue nor of Saracen tongue....If anyone recites it well in the French manner, I think that great profit will accrue to him from so doing and that it will be manifest to him in this life....I heard it read by young clerks and by learned men, excellent men, even as the Passion shows it, in which these lessons are read. And if our melody pleases you, as the first mode guides it, I will sing it to you for nothing.'

The poet has heard a reading from a Latin life of the saint, perhaps in more than one version, a recitation given 'under a pine tree'. This probably does not mean 'out in the woods', as the editor suggests; the pine tree was a regular ornament of the court of a castle or monastery; it usually sheltered the stone or steps at which visitors dismounted when about to enter the building; e.g. *Guibert d'Andrenas*, l. 1030, 'Et descendirent soz lo pin verdoiant'. *Jourdain de Blaivies*, l. 41, 'Desoz le pin au perron descendie'. *Doon de la Roche*, 'le pin au perron', ll. 3999, 4278, 4337. *Girart de Roussillon*, l. 6274, 'Dun Mile parle au porter desoz un sap', during the sack of the castle. The olive tree also appears in the same connection: *Aliscans*, l. 2027; *La Chevalerie Vivien*, l. 1042; *Raoul de Cambrai*, l. 827. Other cases could be mentioned. The reading thus may have taken place at the entrance to a monastery, the readers relieving one another in turns; as a knowledge of Latin was required, the audience would be chiefly clerical. The poet, observing the interest aroused by the legend, thinks that a version produced 'a lei francesca' should be successful; he wrote in Provençal, the term 'francesca' covering languages other than those mentioned in the preceding lines. He then departs and proceeds to construct his version upon the basis of his memory of the Latin legend.

His production is a complete contrast to the Anglo-Norman poem on Sainte Foi, by Simon de Walsingham, who followed very closely the Latin text of the *Passion*. 'Son récit est tout autre chose qu'une traduction, ou même une adaptation libre de ses modèles latins....Sans doute, il y a des passages où il suit de très près les textes latins... mais ces passages sont courts et relativement rares. Ils ne forment qu'une infime partie de son œuvre. En général, il procède avec une liberté souveraine; il taille hardiment dans la matière; il la modifie selon les besoins de la cause et traite les données traditionnelles avec une désinvolture étonnante' (Hoepffner, p. 235). This is just what might be expected, if he wrote from memory of what he had heard.

The process of circulation might have proceeded as follows. A new epic or *roman* is produced and recited by the author or by a jongleur in his service; success is immediate and the reciter obtains no small advantage in the matter of gifts, presents, invitations and reputation. Other jongleurs see no reason why this iniquitous monopoly should be preserved; the only method of breaking it is to produce the same thing themselves. The owner is not likely to lend them his copy. Therefore, one or two of them contrive to be present at as many recitations as they can attend, and proceed to construct their own versions upon a memory basis.[1] So long as the use of the poem is confined to a narrow circle, receipts are likely to remain at a fairly high level; but others are equally anxious for a share of the profits and secure command of the text by the same methods. By this time the original text has been pretty thoroughly 'corrupted', to use the editorial term; the sequence of incident, the conversations, descriptions and arguments are more or less preserved, but the stock phrases, the rime sequence, and other details of the kind are varied by individual reproducers. It may even happen that a jongleur re-edits the whole work to suit the kind of audience that he usually attracts (e.g. the versions of *Flore et Blancheflore*). Some of these copies disappear; others are recopied by scribes whose variations of method and accuracy produce further divergence. When the modern editor is confronted with the remnants, the wreckage and the flotsam which the seas of time have washed up to the shore of modernity, what is he to do with them? The difficulty is well stated by a writer[2] attempting to relate three fragments of *Erec et Enide* to the manuscript tradition:

'To summarise, then, it must be said that none of the three fragments of *Erec et Enide* can be assigned with assurance to any one MS. family. *Th* and *G* are too short. *An*, like *G*, is at least long enough to exemplify almost every type of textual problem and perplexity, and, as related to *Erec*, to show results akin to those obtained from study of the text as a whole, i.e. that no entirely clear-cut and uncontaminated families can be

1 So, in Elizabethan times, 'pirates' attended the playhouse in order to get what they could by listening.

2 Jean Misrahi, *Fragments of Erec et Enide*, P.M.L.A. LVI (December 1941), p. 958.

posited. The evidence points either to considerable and almost systematic individualism on the part of each scribe or else to equally considerable and crisscross "contamination" of all the MSS. Until we have more direct knowledge of the habits and procedures of medieval scribes occupied in copying vernacular texts, we cannot definitely know. It seems probable, however, that both sources of MS. variation were ever present in varying degree. The "mechanical" sources of scribal errors, as exposed by Vinaver,[1] are responsible for only an infinitesimal fraction of the total number of variants in any text of which we have several MSS. As yet we know with certainty only that the MSS. very frequently disagree. Until we know why in each individual case, or, in other words, until we can see the reason for each textual variation, any method that we may use to tabulate them with a view to establishing distinct "families" of MSS. is foredoomed to failure. That we shall ever have such knowledge seems unlikely. Accordingly, the surest and most realistic method of editing a text would seem to be to choose very carefully a "base" MS. and reproduce it in its entirety, excepting when it gives a reading that is obviously nonsense and when it is reasonably certain 'what the *scribe* intended to write.'

If we regard oral tradition as an additional source of 'contamination' we have a fairly complete account of the amount and kind of variation with which editors of texts have to reckon. Hence, in many cases, methods of editing formerly in vogue have been abandoned. Textual criticism to within recent times has been dominated by the classical and biblical criticism which developed its methods before the criticism of medieval texts had fully begun. A reaction has now set in.[2]

The production of literature was largely dependent upon patronage. Froissart, for instance, gives a lengthy list of the royal personages and

1 For a recent and clear exposition of the various sorts of 'mechanical' scribal errors see Eugene Vinaver's study on the *Principles of Textual Emendation*, in *Studies in French Language and Mediaeval Literature Presented to Professor M. K. Pope*, Manchester University Press, 1939, pp. 351–70.

2 See Appendix D. Editors of Chaucer's *Canterbury Tales* are confronted with MS. variations of such a character as to justify the use of the term 'chaotic' in estimating the relationship and value of the several MSS. Heroic efforts have been made to discover some principle of priority or order. Editors who discuss 'scribal confusion' might well find an explanation of it in a previous stage of oral transmission.

nobles who had befriended him.[1] The troubadour gained the favour of some noble or of his lady, was attached to his court, provided with a livelihood and with rewards, because his songs brought reputation and renown to his patron. He was also useful for political purposes; the *sirventes* was a poetical form constructed as the love song, and concerned with social or political satire; these songs broadcasted by jongleurs were passed from mouth to mouth, and, as what we call 'news' was scarce and slow in transit, exercised a considerable influence upon general opinion. The political sirventes of Bertran de Born are well known; the personal sirventes of Guillem de Berguedan rival the best efforts of Dr Goebbels. International propaganda was disseminated by these methods; in 1285 Pedro III of Aragon, when threatened with war by Philip III of France, attempted to arouse sympathy for himself among the courts North of the Pyrenees by an interchange of stanzas with poets of French loyalty. Productions that can be described only as lampoons were also circulated. In the Galician school[2] they had become a recognised genre, *cantigas de escarnho et maldizer*, by which means disgruntled nobles as well as insignificant *trovadores* were wont to vent their spleen upon any subject or person arousing their disapproval. Alfonso el Sabio, following the lead of certain towns in Spain, where the practice had become a menace, legislated against it in his *Siete Partidas*; the text refers to libellous action 'non tan solamente por palabra, mas aun por escripturas faciendo cantigas, o rimas o dictados malos'; action is either public or secret, 'echando aquellas escripturas malas en las casas de los grandes señores, o en las iglesias, o en las plazas comunales de las cibdades, de las villas, porque cada uno lo pueda leer'. Written libel is worse than spoken slander, 'porque dura la remembranza della para siempre si la escriptura no se pierde'. Alfonso thus seems to have in view not only *cantigas* in recognised form, but other kinds of lampoon which might be in verse or in any form likely to remain in the minds of those who read and heard them. This fashion of disseminating slander has been common in all societies and at all times; Pietro Aretino and his pasquinades naturally come to mind as an obvious example. Giraut Riquier constantly inveighs against the blackmailing joglar who will speak evil, if he is not rewarded to his liking; and the written is, as Alfonso considered, worse than the spoken word:

1 *Le Buisson de Jonece* (1366), ed. Buchon, III, p. 500.
2 Anglade, *Le troubadour Giraut Riquier*, Paris, 1905, p. 163.

Pero mais a de brieu
Malditz de trobadors,
Que si so a lauzors,
Car tot es sagelat.[1]

The practice of dropping lampoons in public or private places, or
fastening them up on walls, suggests that the perpetrator of the libel
could count upon someone who would read his production and circulate at least the substance of it, if not the text. The question of the
number of people in average society able to read has been previously
discussed. Alfonso and Riquier were speaking at the close of the thirteenth century, when literacy was more common than in the eleventh
or twelfth centuries.

In any case, public opinion was regarded from very early times as a
force with which everyone of social standing had to reckon. A man's
reputation was as dear to him as his life. Roland exhorts his com-
panions:

Or guart chascuns que granz colps i empleit
Que malvaise cancum de nus chantet ne seit.[2]

To be pointed at (*estre au doi mostré*) was bad enough, but the lampoon
went from mouth to mouth and suggested additional gossip. Satire of
this kind circulated in many armies; Caesar himself was not exempt as
a subject of song. When Count Ebles hid himself from a sortie of
Northmen during the siege of Chartres, his cowardice was stigmatised
in this manner:

Vers en firent e estraboz
Ci out assez de vilains moz.

Richard was vilified by Henry, duke of Burgundy, during the Third
Crusade, 'et la chançon par l'ost hanta'. This anxiety to maintain a
reputation is found in most civilisations and ages; Odysseus regrets,
when in danger of shipwreck, that he had not died before Troy, 'for
then the Achaeans would have spread my fame, but now it is my fate
to be caught by a shameful death'.[3] But in a feudal society, continually
agitated by petty jealousies and rivalries, in which loyalty to the over-

1 Mahn, *Werke*, III, p. 194.
2 *Chanson de Roland*, 1013; see Jenkins' note, and also Wilmotte, *L'Epopée
française*, p. 150, who gives other instances. *Aliscans*, l. 453 d.
3 *Od.* v, 310.

lord was the only permanent bond, and in which suspicion of disloyalty might have fatal results, slander and gossip was a danger that could not be disregarded. It was a danger increased by the fact that many people of social standing often had a good deal of time on their hands and little to occupy their minds. In the absence of news from the outer world, the affairs of their immediate neighbours were naturally of absorbing interest. There was the further fact, that in medieval life there was very little privacy; except in the case of the castle lord and his wife, there were no private rooms for the majority of those attached to his service. Hence the continual references in lyric poetry to slanderers and backbiters, the 'lausengier bec esmolut', which the Monk of Montaudon counts among his 'annoyances'; hence also the stress laid upon silence and secrecy as an essential part of a lover's service. If two people were attracted to one another, a word or a look might become the starting-point of rumours vexatious or even dangerous to those concerned. If the printing press can spread these more widely and certainly, the author of them can be more readily identified, and is therefore more careful of the consequences.

The observations on the subject made in the *Leys d'Amors*[1] probably represent public opinion in the first half of the fourteenth century. 'Satire of a private character (*mal digz especials*) occurs when, in a *sirventes* or other work, ill is said of any individual. For no one should be mentioned by name in works, nor should composers of satire say such words as can be applied to any particular person. This does not mean that people in general may not be satirised, but they should not be mentioned by name. Classes and professions may be the subject of satire; no one can object to this, as the object of satire is to correct vice; an objector is therefore liable to admit his own culpability.'

The patron therefore regarded the jongleur or minstrel as something more than an expensive luxury. He could make or mar a reputation; he could spread the fame of his employer; Charles d'Anjou attempted to counteract the unpopularity of his rule in Sicily by employing Adam de la Hale to compose a laudation of 400 lines, the *Dit du roi de Sicile*. Roger of Hovenden relates that Bishop Longchamp, who was chancellor of England during the absence of Richard Cœur de Lion, hired jongleurs to sing his praises in public: 'hic ad augmentum et famam sui nominis emendicata carmina et rhythmos adulatorios comparabat et de

1 Ed. Gatien-Arnoult, III, p. 125.

regno Francorum cantores et joculatores muneribus allexerat, ut de illo canerent in plateis et jam dicebatur ubique, quod non erat talis in orbe'. Henry I threatened to put out the eyes of the captured minstrel Luc de la Barre for composing *estrabots* satirising the throne. A statute of Sarum warns church people against minstrels with their *laude, immo verius fraude*, and their *detractationibus*. Family chronicles were also produced by jongleurs for their patrons. The exploits of William Longsword at the battle of Mansourah in 1250 were recorded in verse:[1]

> Ky vodra de doel e de͛ pite oier tres graunt
> De bon William Long-Espee, ly hardy combatant etc.

The History of William the Marshal, who was regent of England from 1216 to 1219 and whose long life saw many important events in English history, was composed by a professional jongleur at the instance of William's eldest son and from materials supplied by him and by others.[2] The work extends to nearly 20,000 lines of octosyllabic verse and was doubtless written in this form for recitation to a family or any other interested audience. Biography in prose is of later date, as has been said.

In the case of these lengthy works, it was usual for the author to prepare a final copy, well transcribed, finely illuminated and bound, for presentation to the patron. This custom seems to have become common in France in the fourteenth century, to judge from the number of miniatures appearing in manuscripts of that period, which represent the author on his knees before his patron, in the act of presenting his work. It has been suggested that this ceremony was equivalent to a formal act of publication.[3] This may have been true in the sense that the author thus abandoned his control of his text, and that anyone was at liberty to copy it with the permission of the patron or other recipient. But such sumptuous volumes might contain works which had been known to the public long before; in 1395 Froissart presented to King Richard II a copy of all the moral and love poems which he had composed during the previous thirty-four years. A public reading before a selected

---

1 S. Bentley, *Excerpta historica, or Illustration of English History*, London, 1831, p. 64; Jubinal, *Nouveau Recueil*, Paris, 1842, II, 339; Fr. Michel, *Mémoires de Jean, sire de Joinville*, Paris, 1858, p. 327.

2 See introduction to P. Meyer's edition, Paris, 1901.

3 R. K. Root, *Publication before Printing*, P.M.L.A. XXVIII (1913), p. 417, who gives some interesting references to Petrarch and Boccaccio.

audience might serve the same purpose of placing the work at the disposal of anyone interested.

Much was also written at the instance of patrons who seem to have had no other motive than an interest in fiction, literature or history, including the narration of their own exploits. According to Wace, who wrote his *Roman de Rou* for Henry II of England, lesser personages were anxious to secure mention of themselves in such histories:

> Cil ki les gestes escriueient
> E ki les estoires faiseient,
> Suuent aueient des baruns
> E des nobles dames beaus duns,
> Pur mettre lur nuns en estoire,
> Que tuz tens mais fust de eus memoire. (ll. 145–150.)

It may have been that the jongleur regarded the satisfaction of such vanity as a source of income for himself; from the patron he would naturally expect a reward. Wace was followed by Benoît de Sainte-Maure, who also wrote for Henry II and dedicated his *Roman de Troie* to Eleanor of Poitiers. So Chrétien de Troyes wrote for Marie de Champagne; Gautier d'Arras for Count Thibaut V of Champagne, and many other cases might be mentioned.

To write a lamentation upon the death of a patron was also among the tasks of the jongleur or troubadour. Among the Provençal troubadours, this lamentation or *planh* was a recognised literary genre. Northern France produced many examples; among the subjects were Louis VIII, William of England, Louis IX and other lesser figures; Rustebuef wrote laments on the king of Navarre, the count of Poitiers and the count of Nevers. Thus the jongleur, among other functions now regarded as the business of the press, performed that of writing obituary notices.

The Puy was an institution which enabled jongleurs to meet and exchange ideas and information. The earliest Puy known to us existed in the South of France and was that in which the troubadour Monk of Montaudon acted as judge: 'e fo faitz seigner de la cort del Puoi Sta Maria, e de dar l'esparvier. Lonc temps ac la seignoria de la cort del Puoi, tro que la cortz se perdet.' This meeting was primarily a tournament, at the conclusion of which poetical competitions were held; it appears to have lasted for some years, as reference is made to it by other troubadours; and as Velay, the place of meeting, was in the possession of Robert I of Auvergne, a well-known patron of troubadours, he may well have been the founder of it. When Northern France began to imitate troubadour lyric poetry, and the taste for it had caught the bourgeois class, Puys were formed in many towns, Paris, Arras, Amiens, Rouen, Abbeville and others, retaining the name and dedication of the original institution. One was also formed in London by the foreign merchants resident or visiting the town. The character of these Puys varied between that of a guild and of a confraternity; the Paris Puy was a guild, maintained with the object of preventing wandering jongleurs from practising their art in Paris and cutting into the home market; other Puys included bourgeois amateurs and, besides cultivating poetry, were in the nature of burial clubs or mutual benefit societies. But the performance of poems in competition formed a regular part of their proceedings. No doubt jongleurs were able at these meetings to exchange information for their mutual benefit; and interchange of items from their repertoire would mean a wider circulation of poetical works.

In the early middle ages the production and distribution of books was chiefly carried on by monastic establishments; copyists and bookdealers working on their own account were not numerous.[1] Peter of Blois was outbid for a parcel of law books which he attempted to secure from a Paris dealer about 1170. Universities controlled the book trade with more or less stringency in the interests of their pupils; this organisation was closer at Paris than elsewhere, probably as a result of the large number of students who resided there. In the fourteenth century the book trade included stationers or writers, booksellers, parchment makers, illuminators and binders. One concern might combine two or three of these avocations. The stationer, so called from the fact that he had a settled place of business and did not travel from town to town, was the medieval counterpart of the modern printer and publisher; he managed the copying of books and employed illuminators to decorate them and binders to finish them when required. The bookseller (*librarius*) sold books or lent them on hire; with this business he might combine the functions of the stationer. The members of this trade were in the position of university officials; they were formally licensed, took an oath to observe university regulations and enjoyed a monopoly

1 Most of the references on this subject are given by Wattenbach, *Das Schriftwesen im Mittelalter*, Leipzig, 1875.

which outside traders could not infringe. As a guarantee of respectability, they had to pay caution money, which might be as much as £200, a very considerable sum in those days. As university officials, they were exempt from municipal jurisdiction and taxation, and had their place in university processions and public functions. They were not allowed to engage in other trades or professions, except those of a literary character—notary, advocate or cleric; in Italy reference is made to them as *bidelli*. The *bidellus* was a public official who acted as town crier, or huissier, in support of the dignity of the municipality; hence probably our university Esquire Bedell.

Books were very expensive, and from the thirteenth century onward the supply never seems to have equalled the demand. Hence the object of a university was to secure the necessary supply of books for its students at the cheapest possible rate. The organisation described was not suddenly imposed upon the trade by the university; it was of gradual growth, emended from time to time in order to secure the object in view. The books required by students were almost entirely concerned with law and theology; the fact that monastic establishments did not usually copy law books, and were in many cases forbidden to do so, gave a stimulus to outside production which became a public trade. The universities were not concerned with contemporary belles-lettres, and producers and sellers of these were probably not interfered with, as they did not infringe the monopoly of legal and theological publication. The stationer who wished to issue a book was obliged to submit it to the university officials, who saw that it was correct and complete and fixed the price of sale. If this regulation may be regarded as containing the germ of copyright law, it was one which protected the purchaser, did nothing for the vendor, except to restrict his profit, and entirely disregarded the existence of the author. The bookseller would not buy unwanted copies, for, if he did, he could sell them only at the taxed price; if he moved elsewhere, he was obliged to leave his stock for his successor, presumably at a valuation. His real profits were gained from the lending of books upon a monetary deposit. Poor students who could not buy a text would pool their resources and buy or hire one for their use during a university session. Books were also lent in sheets, *peciae*, and the copying of these or of whole books by students was a practice both regular and encouraged. Public and, under conditions, monastic libraries were also accessible for study or for copyists.

During the two centuries before the invention of printing, independent booksellers increased in number. Richard of Bury, the author of *Philobiblon* and bishop of Durham, bought books in France, Germany and Italy; he spoke eloquently of the advantages of Paris for the book collector: 'ibi virens viridarium universorum voluminum'. In England the book trade was more independent of the universities than on the continent; the London stationers had formed the inevitable guild by 1403, and had established themselves in the vicinity of St Paul's, where they remained until German barbarism recently destroyed their establishments. It was to such booksellers that customers would go who wanted literature other than law or theology, and the demand for such literature grew steadily, as it was bound to do with the spread of education. Even theologians and lawyers require some relaxation; as the middle classes increased in wealth and importance, they discovered the necessity of education for business purposes and saw that their children were taught to read and write; so a demand for popular literature became steadily more general. Book prices were also lowered by the discovery of rag paper, and the invention of mechanical means of reproduction was the natural sequel. A very cursory examination of early *incunabula* will show that the printer did his best to reproduce the text in manuscript form; there will be no title nor titlepage, the scribe's abbreviations will be reproduced, his proportion of text to margin observed and so on. There is some reason to believe that the primitive printed text was regarded by the reading public with a certain contempt, as electro-plate is considered in comparison with silver. Fashions change and many *incunabula* are now more expensive than any existing manuscript of the text which they reproduce. However, these are matters concerning the history of the printed book, and our subject ends where this history begins.

CHAPTER VII

CONCLUSION

FEW historians would care to contest Bacon's statement that the inventions of printing, gunpowder and the mariner's compass have changed the form of civilisation, and all would probably agree that he placed these inventions in the order of their relative importance. While much has been written upon the importance of printing as accelerating the diffusion of culture and knowledge, few attempts have been made to contrast the mental attitude of the scholar and the literary man in the ages before print with that of the reading and writing public when print had superseded manuscript as a medium for communicating ideas. The difference is that between the medieval and the modern world. Book collectors have agreed to regard 1500 as the date after which *incunabula* begin to lose their scarcity value and their interest as illustrating the development of the printer's art. This choice of date is arbitrary and somewhat misleading; printing began later in some countries than in others, and in Spain, for instance, the dividing line might be placed some thirty or forty years later. But in 1492 Columbus made his great voyage, in 1494 Charles VIII invaded Italy, in 1500 Copernicus was lecturing in Rome, Erasmus and Luther were at work and in 1521 the Diet of Worms was held, while in the previous year Magelhaēs had circumnavigated the globe. In the effects of such events the difference between medieval and modern is apparent, in the enlargement of outlook upon the world and the interpretation of man's place and powers in it. That extension of view would have unfolded much more slowly than it did, if the printer had not already been at work for half a century.

What picture, then, can be drawn of a man of letters, of his culture and capacity in medieval times? As a text, we may take the eulogy composed by Guittone d'Arezzo,[1] who was born about the middle of the thirteenth century:

> Tu frate mio, vero bon trovatore
> in piana e'n sottile rima e chiara

1 Monaci, *Crestomazia Italiana*, p. 184.

e in soavi e saggi e chari motti,
Francesca lingua e Proensal labore
più de l'Ar(e)tina è bene in te, che chiara
la parlasti e trovasti in modi totti.

Such a man would have read but little and that little very slowly, in comparison with modern erudition, but his memory was neither overloaded nor impaired; he could not comfort his soul with the reflection that facts and dates were to be found in books of reference within reach of his arm. He probably knew such of the Latin classics as were then available, had studied the precepts of the medieval rhetoricians and could compose in the simple or obscure and difficult style, with obvious or far-fetched rimes. He knew both French and Provençal, had doubtless read or heard the best known epic and lyric poems, and, like many of his compatriots, could produce a *roman d'aventure* in French of a sort, and a love song in conventional Provençal. But the choice of language was decided for him, as was the choice of style, by the nature of the subject-matter, and if he wished to compose, free from the need of keeping a wary eye upon rules and conventions, his native dialect offered a freer scope. He possessed no final standard of linguistic scholarship, in our sense of the term; no language in which he dealt had been finally stabilised; his only standard of correctness was current usage and his only purpose to interest or amuse his hearers. His knowledge of the historical past was confused with legendary and fabulous elements, and his knowledge of current events was derived from hearsay, local gossip, or

Joglars de moutas manieras
Que tot jorn van per las carieiras
Cantan, trepan e baorden,
E van bonas novas dizen
E las proessas e las guerras
Que son faichas en autres terras,[1]

unless he happened to have access to official and governmental circles. Such a man probably did not expect fame or more than temporary profit from any work that he might produce. The author, in medieval times, was little accounted of. The great bulk of narrative poetry remains anonymous; the lyric poet had more chance of establishing a personal

1 *Jaufre*, ed. Breuer, Göttingen, 1925, ll. 3077 ff. (date, 1225–30).

reputation, because his jongleurs would advertise his name and because of the personal appeal in much that he wrote. But, in general, the medieval public was not greatly interested in the personality of the author. Modern ideas on this matter are in direct contrast with those of medieval days. The name of a well-known author is now regarded as a guarantee of the kind of book that may be expected from him; his style and mode of dealing with his subject are regarded as a revelation of his personality and readers are attracted as much by his manner as by his matter. In the same way, theatre-goers are interested quite as much in the actors who perform a drama as in the play itself.

The medieval listener had a greater respect for form than for authorship. The rules for telling a story had been laid down by the rhetoricians and the composer of narrative poetry was expected to conform to them. The lyric love poem was based upon a principle of tripartition, as expounded by Dante in the *De Vulgari Eloquentia*, and this principle could not be ignored. But, provided that these fundamental rules were observed, the author had free scope for his imagination and ingenuity. He could complicate his tale with incident and episode or adorn his lyric with ingenious turns of expression and unusual rimes. But genius could not run wild; poetry was a science and inspiration could not replace training and practice. Few compositions have gained more appreciation in modern times than *Aucassin et Nicolette*; but this *chantefable* is unique of its kind, and if we ask why it was not imitated, the answer may be that imitations of it have perished; but it is also possible that such a departure from the norm was not appreciated by medieval conservatism.

Something of the same spirit is apparent in medieval architecture. A cathedral must have certain essential features demanded by use and purpose; certain laws of structure must be observed by the builders, if the edifice is not to collapse. But within these limits great freedom of design was possible; the Gothic architects could revel in traceried windows, lofty decorative arches, ranks of crocketed pinnacles, elaborate mouldings and carvings, decoration in glass and stone. It is more than a coincidence that the same spirit can be observed in Gothic script, which was almost universally employed by scribes for some three centuries, and was evolved from the Caroline minuscule during the later years of the twelfth century. The fundamental requirements for a script are legibility and economy of space, in view of the expense of parchment. These needs were fairly met by the Caroline script, but scribes began to 'improve' it; hooks, flourishes and other adornments became fashionable and eventually produced the angular Gothic, not nearly so legible as the Caroline, but more pleasing to the eye in the earnest consistency of its style and the compactness of its line. The Renaissance produced the humanistic minuscule, and the adoption of it by the printers eventually overpowered the Gothic; but Gothic held its ground for a considerable time and is not yet out of use in Germany.

These artistic tendencies were consistent with the political and religious philosophy of the middle ages. It was a philosophy based upon a belief in the principle of harmony which an earthly society may maintain by faith in God and by the pursuit of righteousness, the active principle of harmony. This principle was held to operate in the physical as well as the moral world; plague and famine, storm and tempest were signs of disharmony in man as well as in nature, an evil resulting from human disregard of a law which was natural, because it was also divine. This idea of an ordered universe, in which moral and physical law were interconnected, provided as much room for variety of religious experience as the architect or the poet enjoyed in his particular sphere; if he violated or neglected the fundamental principles of his art, confusion would result, and, if human pride or selfishness outraged the divine and natural principle, physical calamity would follow moral transgression. Hence it was the business of authority to maintain this principle of harmony between the physical and the moral world, the human and the divine; 'propter quod opus fuit homini duplici directivo, secundum duplicem finem: scilicet summo Pontifice, qui secundum revelata humanum genus perduceret ad vitam aeternam; et Imperatore, qui secundum philosophica documenta genus humanum ad temporalem felicitatem dirigeret'.[1]

1 Dante, *De Monarchia*, ad fin.

APPENDIX A

Medieval Literature, written to be recited and primitive in character, naturally preserved certain syntactical mannerisms which were eliminated in the course of progress towards literary style, a process accelerated when individual reading became an amusement and the age of printing began. Early language is inclined to avoid subordinate clauses; the elaboration of the Ciceronian period is but little attempted, for the reason that auditors with acoustic, but with no visualising capacity, are likely to lose the thread of a lengthy sentence, unless it is presented to them in co-ordinate clauses. Hence we find loosely constructed sentences, either united by overworking the useful particles *que* and *si*, or put together without connection (asyndeton) in the assurance that the tone and emphasis given by the reciter will secure comprehension of the author's meaning. *Pitet l'en prent, ne poet muer n'en plurt*, is equivalent to a principal followed by a consecutive clause: 'such grief comes over him, that he cannot help weeping', and the hearer will instinctively draw this conclusion. If this possibility is doubtful, *et* may be used to mark the principal clause:

> Que tan l'am de bon coratge,
> c'ades soi entredormitz
> et ab lui ai guidonatge. (Peire d'Alvernhe.)

'For I love him so dearly that at once I fall asleep and I have his presence', i.e. as soon as I fall asleep, etc.

> Tantost con la lur mostra, e cascuna s'estent.
> (*Vida de Saint Honorat.*)

'As soon as the saint shows the serpents the cross, *then* each of them is stretched out dead.' Editors who attempt to amend this use out of existence probably regard it as an archaism; but it is common enough. The Latin *simul ac*, translated 'as soon as', is a parallel case (cp. also *Fors et*, Virgil, *Aen.* ii, 139, 'there is a chance that', i.e. 'probably').

Que can be used to indicate a causal, concessive, consecutive or final connection; if ambiguity is likely, *que* can be qualified, *per que*, *abans que*, *tro que*, etc., but the reader or audience are often left to interpret the connection for themselves. *Si* as adverb (Lat. *sic*) is also loosely used; it may emphasise the subject of a sentence; *lo vescoms si avia moiller*, 'the viscount, he had a wife'; *lo monges si fo gentils hom*, 'the monk, he was of noble birth'. It may be used as adversative:

> mais regina vera
> no sai el mon, e si n'ai mainta quista. (Peire Vidal.)

'A truer queen I know not in the world, and yet I have sought many a one.'
It may mark the apodosis of the sentence:

> si mon cor sabia,
> s'era la peier qu'el mon sia,
> si.l penria de mi merces.   (Amanieu de Sescas.)

'If she knew my heart, if she were the worst woman that there is in the world,
then
yet pity for me would come upon her.' In such phrases as the adjurations
si m'aiut Dieus; si te veyas logrado,[1] usage has obscured the difference between
Latin *si* and *sic*.

This tendency to the use of asyndeton diminished, as the language became
more literary and a system of connecting particles was developed. The history
of declension might be traced as proceeding under similar influences. We often
read in the introduction to a thirteenth-century text, 'declension is neglected',
a feature which becomes more pronounced as time goes on. 'Neglect' was due
to the fact that noun inflexions were not always written, unless they were meant
to be heard; the author had no respect for visual grammatical accuracy as such;
he wanted to be understood and any method of securing this end commended
itself to him. When the discovery was made that clarity and emphasis could be
obtained by the use of prepositions followed by the accusative case, the original
system of noun declension was doomed.

The inconsistency of tense usage in narrative passages may be explicable upon
the same principles. Take the passage quoted by Foulet (*Petite Syntaxe*, 1919,
p. 159; *La Chastelaine de Vergi*, ll. 728 ff.):

> Dedenz une garderobe *entre*
> ou une pucelete *estoit*
> qui aus piez du lit se *gisoit*,
> mes ele ne la *pot* veoir.
> El lit *s'est lessie* cheoir
> la chastelaine mout dolente;
> iluec *se plaint* et *se demente*,
> et *dist*: 'Ha! sire Dieus, merci!'

The salient points in the narrative are that the *châtelaine* entered the room in a
state of great distress; these are described in the present tense in order to bring
the scene directly before the imagination of the audience. The imperfect tenses
are quite natural, as is the preterite in line 4. The compound tense is used to
emphasise the action preliminary to the act of weeping; possibly the reciter
went through the action himself. The preterite in the last line starts a fresh stage

1 *Libro de Apolonio*, 409 c.

in the action, explanatory of the description previously given. In other words, we have to consider what points the reciter wishes to impress upon his audience, and what means he might have employed to secure his end, if we are to understand his use of tenses. Foulet's comment, 'on paraît surtout chercher la variété', is equivalent to giving up the problem as hopeless. If we regard such poems as intended for our private armchair reading, the problem *is* hopeless.

APPENDIX B

Further examples of *lire* in the sense of 'to read aloud', whether to oneself or to an audience, which also are evidence of literacy or illiteracy, are the following:

La Vie Seint Edmund le Rei, poème anglo-normand du XIIe siècle, par Denis Piramus, ed. H. Kjellman, Göteborg, 1935, ll. 43 ff.

> E si en aiment mult l'escrit
> E lire le funt, si unt delit,
> E si las funt sovent retreire.
> Les lais solent as dames pleire,
> De joie les oient e de gré.

In Beroul's *Tristran*, the letter to King Mark, offering reconciliation, is written by the hermit Ogrin (l. 2428), its content being dictated by Tristran. The king is unable to read it and the chaplain is called upon:

> Dan chapelain, lisiez le brief,
> oiant nos toz, de chief en chief.   (l. 2547.)

The chaplain is also ordered to write an answer:

> Li rois son chapelain apele:
> 'Soit fait cist brief o main isnele;
> Oï avez que i metroiz.'   (l. 2639.)

Letters from Northern Registers, Rolls Series, London, 1873, p. 302:

Quibus literis coram Concilio ejusdem domini nostri regis lectis et examinatis, videbatur eidem Concilio etc.   (Date, 1320.)

Tanquerey, *Lettres Anglo-françaises*, p. 153:

Quelles lettres leues et entendues, il semble a moi etc.   (Date, 1330.)

Ibid. p. 160:

As toutz yceux qe cestes lettres verront ou orront, etc.   (Date, 1350.)

Ibid. p. 99:

Pour ceo, sire, que vous orrez bones noveles de moun seignur le rey et ma dame la reyne, vous fas a saver etc.   (Date, 1311.)

And p. 59:

Sire, jo rescu vostre lettre...et entendi ben par vos letres ke vus ne avez pas volente de grever les Freres. (Date, 1289.)

The usual phrase is 'desirant de oir et savoir de vos nouvelles'. It is difficult to say whether such formulae imply inability to read, or to read silently, any more than the modern phrase, 'I have not heard from him for some time', meaning, 'I have had no letter'. Or is 'hear' in this modern sense a survival from medieval use?

Such a survival seems to be the use of the terms 'audit' and 'auditor' with reference to the scrutiny and verification of accounts, which have become obsolete in modern French and point to a time when 'auditing' was as much a matter of ears as of eyes. In the treatise of Thomas de Eccleston, *De Adventu Minorum* (Rolls Series, *Monumenta Franciscana*, London, 1858, p. 8), we find 'accidit ut Frater Angnellus...vellet audire compotum fratrum Londoniae, quantum sc. expendissent infra unum terminum anni, cumque audisset quod tam sumptuose processisset vel satis parca fratrum exhibitio, projecit omnes talias et rotulos, et percutiens seipsum in faciem, exclamavit, "Ay me captum!" et nunquam postea voluit audire compotum'. Thomas wrote in the latter half of the thirteenth century; more than a century later, the same terms were in use in Anglo-Norman. Alice, Countess of Kent, wrote to her 'auditour' after 1397, asking him to examine the accounts of Sir H. Mory, clerk of the household to her late husband; 'pur ce que sire H. Mory...soy purpose pur rendre son accompte de l'office avauntdit...c'est assavoir par un an entier, de quel il est soulement accomptable, vous mandons en priantz que vous vous ordeignez d'oier les accomptz del dit sire H. come nostre auditour' (*Anglo-Norman Letters and Petitions*, ed. M. Dominica Legge, Oxford, 1941, p. 268). The term 'countur' was also used; see F. J. Tanquerey, *Lettres Anglo-françaises*, Paris, 1916, p. 28, in a letter of date 1276–82: 'au quel jour vint sire Johan de Lovetot...e mustra par le counturs le roy devaunt nus ke le avant dit sire Bones out une bulle purchacé...'.

In *Le Roman du Comte d'Anjou* (date 1316, given by the author, Jehan Maillart), where the plot of the story depends largely upon letters written, sent, falsified, undelivered and forged, evidence on literacy is more copious than usual:

l. 3110. Sez lectres fet tantost escrire.

l. 3241. Li chastelainz...a fet unnes lectres escrire.

l. 3396. La contesse...unne autre lectre a fet escrire Par un sien frere chappe-lain.

l. 3576. The count, who is literate, instructs the messenger: 'unnes lectres porteras Escriptes de ma proppre main'.

l. 3660. The countess 'fist la lectre effacier, Puis i fist escrire arriere Faussement en ceste menniere'.

l. 3921. The Chastelain orders the executioners to kill the countess and her child. On their refusal, 'tenes, fet il, veez la lectre. Quant il ont la lectre veue N'i a celi qui ne tressue D'angoisse etc.' They understand the meaning.

l. 4823. The Chastelain denies to the Count that he sent such letters 'ne ne les fiz faire; j'en puis mon clerc a garant traire Qui lez lectres fist de sa main'. The clerk examines the letter: 'Ha! dist il, male flambe l'arde Qui c'escript! Ce ne fiz je pas...si n'est ce pas ci mon escript' (l. 4854).

Thus the heads of a large seigneurial household might or might not be literate; they usually kept a clerk who could do what writing was needed, and probably also kept the estate accounts.

The poems of Froissart provide some instances of *lire* for non-silent reading; quotations are from the edition by A. Scheler, Bruxelles, 1870.

L'Espinette Amoureuse, ll. 696 ff.:

> Droitement sus l'eure de prime,
> S'esbatoit une damoiselle
> Au lire un rommant; moi vers elle
> M'en vinc et li dis doucement:
> 'Par son nom ce rommant, comment
> L'apellés vous, ma belle et douce?'
> Elle cloï atant la bouche;
> Sa main dessus le livre adoise.
> Lors respondi, comme courtoise,
> Et me dist: 'De Cleomades
> Est appellés';

L'Espinette Amoureuse, ll. 1287 ff.:

> 'J'ai ci escript une chançon;
> Par amours vœillés le moi lire.'
> Et ma dame prist lors a rire,
> Qui tost pensa dont ce venoit,
> Et dist: 'Ça!' Quant elle le voit,
> Souef en basset le lisi;
> De sa bouche riens el n'issi
> Fors tant, par maniere de glose:
> 'Ce qu'il demande, c'est grant chose!'

In line 1288 *moi* is 'ethic', and reinforces *par amours*: 'read it, if you please'; not, 'read it to me', which would be unnecessary, as the speaker was the composer. Lines 1293-4 state that the lady read it with only so much pronunciation as was needed to make it intelligible to herself.

La Prison Amoureuse, ll. 3421 ff.:

> Et quant j'oi leü une espasse
> Le livret, que riens n'i trespasse,

Moult me samblerent en lisant
Li parler nouvel et plaisant,
Et si volontiers les ooie
Que partir je ne m'en pooie.

Ibid. ll. 3707 ff.:

Le signet rompi, puis les œvre
Et les lisi de cief en cor.
A ce que puis veoir encor,
Rose m'escript con amis chiers
Nouvelles que j'oi volentiers
Et qui pas ne font a celer.

The Beghards or Beguines were founded by one Lambert, who was a popular preacher in Liége from about 1167 to 1191; he was known as 'le Bègue', 'the Stammerer', whence the name applied to his followers. From this name was copied the term 'Lollard', early in the fourteenth century, which is derived from the Flemish, *lollen* or *lullen*, to mutter or mumble. Beghard was soon confused with the English 'beggar', with which it has no connection, and ecclesiastics derived 'Lollard' from *lolium*, the tares among the wheat, while the unlearned derived it from the English *loll*, to lounge or sprawl about (Deanesly, *Lollard Bible*, pp. 69–70). Latin writers who refer to the point use the term *ruminare*. It is not easy to see why popular preachers should be characterised as stammerers or mutterers; it may be that their habit of reading vernacular copies of the scriptures to themselves in public places, without having learnt the art of silent reading, suggested the nickname.

For non-silent writing, Martin Luther gives evidence in his *Predigt, das man Kinder zur Schule halten solle* (1530):

Es meinen wohl etliche, das Schreiberamt sei ein leicht geringes Amt.... Leicht ist die Schreibfeder, das ist wahr; ist auch kein Handzeug unter allen Handwerken bass zu erzeugen denn das der Schreiberei; denn sie bedarf allein der Gänse Fittich, der man umsonst allenthalben genug findet. Aber es muss gleichwohl das beste Stücke (als der Kopf) und das edelste Glied (als die Zunge) und das höchste Werk (als die Rede), so am Menschenleibe sind, hier herhalten und am meisten arbeiten.

APPENDIX C

Rimes for the eye or visual rimes are due in part to tradition, preserved by the printed language. Pronunciation changes, while orthography remains fixed, and rimes that once were perfect and are now false are allowed by poetic usage to remain, provided that the tradition is supported by identity of spelling; thus Shelley could write:

> Lured by the *love* of the genii that *move*
> In the depths of the purple sea.

A further excuse is found in the fact that English is a language poor in rimes, as compared with many other languages. French is inclined to run to the opposite extreme; rimes acoustically correct are banned, if they are orthographically different: *nous—loup, bonté—chantez* and the like, though homophonous in modern pronunciation, are regarded as incorrect. This is a tradition from pre-seventeenth-century pronunciation, when final consonants were sounded; but exceptions can be found as early as La Fontaine, and modern poets allow themselves considerable freedom in this respect.

The controversy upon the value of rime as enhancing or hindering poetical effect has been going on since Trissino attacked rime at the outset of the sixteenth century. Most French critics agree with Voltaire, that blank verse in French is a failure, because it is indistinguishable from prose. This assertion probably refers to recited verse; if unrimed alexandrines were printed as prose, the reader would speedily discover the fact; a recitation in a strong 'sing-song' manner might also betray it. But French, being a *langue homotone*, cannot do without rime, as can languages with a strongly marked stress accent. However, this matter and the relation of rime vowels to the musical scale, on which much has been written, are outside of our subject. A book which summarises previous discussions and adds some new information is *The Physical Basis of Rime*, H. Lanz (Stanford University Press, 1931); it also contains a useful bibliography.

APPENDIX D

Textual criticism, in the modern sense of the term, is usually considered to have been founded by the work of Karl Lachmann (1793–1851); he was chiefly occupied with classical and Old or Middle High German texts, though he also produced an edition of the New Testament in 1842. To the end of the eighteenth century critics were employed chiefly in discovering MSS. and in recording variant readings; they were inclined to rely upon the principle that in the multitude of counsellors is wisdom and, in the case of Biblical literature, to accept any reading supported by a considerable number of MSS., provided that it did not contradict theological orthodoxy. This was the only principle that governed the editing of classical texts; the preface, for instance, of H. A. J. Munro's edition of Lucretius describes a state of uncritical muddle which may be regarded as typical of the ages before Lachmann. Lachmann showed the possibility of classifying MSS. in families by noting the variants or mistakes common to particular MSS.; the obvious inference followed, that the antiquity of a MS. was an important factor in the estimate of its evidential value, and that the coincident testimony of two different groups was more cogent than that of one. The use of such metaphorical terms as 'family' and 'affinity' naturally suggested the idea of genealogy; and editors were expected to produce a genealogical tree, showing their conception of the relations between the MSS. in which the works which they studied had been transmitted, and justifying the choice of those MSS. on which the texts were to be based. The principle is stated by Westcott and Hort in their introduction to the New Testament in Greek: 'all trustworthy restoration of corrupted texts is founded on the study of their history, that is, of the relations of descent or affinity which connect the several documents.... The use of genealogical evidence... involves three successive processes. First, the analysis and comparison of the documentary evidence for a succession of individual variations; next, the investigation of the genealogical relations between the documents; and thirdly, the application of these genealogical relations to the interpretation of the documentary evidence for each individual variation.'

These principles were, not unnaturally, adopted by the early nineteenth-century editors of medieval texts. Some of these editors had been brought up in the classical tradition; they saw that Lachmann's methods produced results which were logically more defensible than the haphazard methods of the previous age. But two difficulties became apparent in course of time. A genealogy cannot be drawn up, unless the approximate dates of the several documents can be established; here the classical or biblical editor has an easier task than the medievalist, because his investigations will extend over centuries of time, whereas the documents transmitting a medieval work may have an ancestry of less than a century; palaeography will help the classical editor to date his MSS. to a far greater extent than it will help the medievalist. The classic can certainly reply, that the longer a work has been in existence, the greater the corruption to which it has been liable; but the difficulties of the medievalist are the same in kind, if less in degree. But there is a more fundamental objection; the comparison between the genealogist and the editor is in the nature of a false analogy. The genealogist is concerned only to show a male line of descent; females are excluded, except for a bare mention of their marriages. In the male line, branches can be represented as divergent, but if female lines were represented in no less detail, convergence would be possible, other aberrations might result, and the genealogical tree would become a confusion rather resembling a bramble-bush. A genealogy of MSS. cannot follow a principle of this kind; genealogy proper depends upon the principle of filiation; the connecting link between a group of MSS. is imitation, which can hardly be regarded as a principle and is subjected to the idiosyncrasies of a succession of scribes.

This genealogical process was attacked by Joseph Bédier in the preface to his edition of *Le Lai de l'Ombre* in 1913 (A.T.F.). Experience of a large number of editions led him to formulate 'une loi, un peu surprenante, qui pourrait se formuler ainsi: Toute entreprise de classement, passée ou future, des manuscrits d'un texte a conduit ou conduira presque fatalement l'opérateur à les repartir en deux familles seulement'. He concluded with the inference, 'on est en présence, non point de faits réels de l'histoire de la transmission des textes, mais à l'ordinaire de phénomènes qui se passent dans l'esprit des éditeurs de textes: auquel cas un nombre indéterminé, mais peut-être considérable, d'éditions de nos anciens textes sont fondées sur des classements erronés en partie et illusoires'. He then abandoned any classification of the six MSS. at his disposal, not from any difficulty in producing a classification, but because he found it possible to produce several, any one of which was as defensible as any other, and he notes the fact that other editors of repute had abandoned Lachmann's methods, if they had not definitely spoken against them. In short, Bédier had the courage to say what other competent scholars had already thought.

At this point, the question was taken up by Dom Henri Quentin (*Essais de Critique Textuelle*, Paris, 1926), a Benedictine occupied with revision of the text of the Vulgate. He objected to the principle of classification upon the basis of common errors; a variant reading is not of necessity an error, unless that term is used in reference to the lost original. A distinction must be made between the terms 'original' and 'archetype', a distinction of terms which Bédier and certainly Gautier do not seem to have consistently observed. A family of MSS. determined as such by readings common to them alone can be referred to one archetype, which, however, may be a long distance from the first original composition and may have inherited from the work of one copyist a series of variations proceeding, for all we know, from some other family intervening between the original and the material which has come down to us. 'Je ne connais ni erreurs, ni fautes communes, ni bonnes ni mauvaises leçons, mais seulement des formes diverses du texte, sur lesquelles, par une méthode qui s'appuie sur des statistiques rigoureuses, je délimite d'abord les familles, puis je classe les manuscrits dans l'intérieur de chacune d'elles, et enfin les familles entre elles. De ce classement résulte un canon critique qui impose pour l'établissement du texte une règle de fer' (p. 37). The result is a text which is as near to the original as is likely to be attained and which is the archetype. Any further corrections will depend upon theological, historical or aesthetic considerations and must be marked in the edition as such. The 'iron rule' is based upon the principle of comparing MSS. in groups of three, with the object of discovering whether any two agree in differing from the third and thus ascertaining which of the three may be regarded as intermediary. The process is much too complicated for description here. Dom Quentin devotes the ninth chapter of his book to an examination of the *Lai de l'Ombre* on the basis of the materials provided by Bédier; the result is a genealogical tree which is identical with that proposed by Bédier in his edition of 1890 and rejected by him in his edition of 1913. It should be noted that Dom Quentin's method professes to give as much weight to agreement between MSS. as to differences between them; his demonstration would therefore be more cogent, if he had subjected the whole poem to his process and not merely 67 lines, of which he omits nine on the ground that they do not contain any variation of interest; for his method insists that all variants, however small, should be taken into account, except those purely orthographical. I do not know whether Bédier expressed any opinion on this demonstration. At the end of his life, he undertook a close examination of various editions of the *Chanson de Roland*, which he summarised in a posthumous article (*Romania*, CCLVI (October 1938), p. 489); here he points out that of the 3998 lines of the Oxford MS., some 1700 passages have been called in question and emended in different ways by different editors, with the result that 'ce texte martyr a subi environ 5000 opérations chirurgicales'. If it is asked how many of these were intended not merely to improve the text, but to restore the readings of the archetype, the number of successes that can be claimed is, in his opinion, twenty-five at least, thirty-five at most.

Thus the modern editor has abandoned the ideal of 'reconstructing the archetype'. There are no fixed rules of procedure which he can follow. The number of MSS. at his disposal, the amount of agreement or disagreement between them, the competence of their copyists, the effect of dialectical differences between the copyists, the possibility of piracy producing divergent imitations, these and other considerations oblige an editor to regard each case as a special case. In the words of Professor A. E. Housman, taken from a paper read to the Classical Association in 1921, 'textual criticism is not a sacred mystery. It is purely a matter of reason and common sense. We exercise textual criticism whenever we notice and correct a misprint. A man who possesses common sense and the use of reason must not expect to learn from treatises or lectures on textual criticism anything that he could not, with leisure and industry, find out for himself. What the lectures and treatises can do for him is to save him time and trouble by presenting to him immediately considerations which would in any case occur to him sooner or later. And whatever he reads about textual criticism in books or hears at lectures, he should test by reason and common sense, and reject everything which conflicts with either as mere hocus-pocus.

Secondly, textual criticism is not a branch of mathematics, nor indeed an exact science at all. It deals with a matter not rigid and constant like lines and numbers, but fluid and variable; namely, the frailties and aberrations of the human mind, and of its insubordinate servants, the human fingers. It is, therefore, not susceptible of hard and fast rules. It would be much easier, if it were; and that is why people try to pretend that it is so, or at least behave as if they thought so. Of course you can have hard and fast rules if you like, but then you will have false rules and they will lead you wrong; because their simplicity will render them inapplicable to problems which are not simple, but complicated by the play of personality. A textual critic engaged upon his business is not at all like Newton investigating the motions of the planets; he is much more like a dog hunting for fleas. If a dog hunted for fleas on mathematical principles, basing his researches on statistics of area and density of population, he would never catch a flea, except by accident. They require to be treated as individuals, and every problem which presents itself to the textual critic must be regarded as possibly unique.'[1]

[1] See also *Modern Philology*, vol. xxviii, *Recent theories of textual criticism*, by W. P. Shepard, p. 129, and W. W. Greg, p. 401.

INDEX

DATE DUE